AMAZING MALAYSIAN

NORMAN MUSA

Amazing Malaysian

RECIPES FOR VIBRANT
MALAYSIAN HOME-COOKING

SQUARE PEG

To my late mum and dad for the unconditional love they gave me
and to Anne, for the beautiful friendship we had.

Contents

AL-HIKMAH SDN. BHD.
TEL: 04-4584048

بسم الله الرحمن الرحيم

ISM

KEDAI

DAN M

4815627

5

ROSES

بسم الله

AH HEE PEMBORONG SAYU
TEL: 012-4330139

AIL

HEE, NASI
INUMAN

NASI LEMAK

Foreword

The first time I went to Malaysia in the early 1980s, I was struck by its amazing cuisine. In the following decades, I had many opportunities to cook with Malaysian chefs not only in Malaysia but also in London. I was consistently impressed by their exquisite palate and love of cooking. Malaysia has always been a crossroad of influences and the ultimate fusion of Malay, Chinese, Indian, Arabic and Portuguese cuisine. My subsequent sojourns back to Malaysia convinced me that it was an underappreciated cuisine and relatively unknown outside of Asia.

So I am thrilled that Norman Musa, a talented restaurant chef, has written this definitive book on Malaysian cookery. Infused with his moving personal accounts of his mother and father's recipes, the book brings to life the glories of Malaysian cuisine with beautiful photographs and mouth-watering dishes. The clear directions and personal guidance in each recipe makes this book a classic and it should be on every serious cook's bookshelf. From street foods and snacks to the wonderful aromatic curries as well as simple stir-fries, you can almost taste the food. There are delectable and original salads and vegetable dishes that are equally satisfying to vegetarians and non-vegetarians. The noodle and rice recipes are both imaginative and creative, while the desserts are a reflection of the richness of the fruit culture of Malaysia.

Norman's book has filled a gap in world food culture and I for one am enormously grateful. Thank you, Norman, for sharing the fabulous cuisine of Malaysia with us!

Ken Hom, OBE

Introduction

I have lived in the UK for 21 years and the thing I miss most about Malaysia is, and always will be, the food. My obsession with recreating the flavours from back home spurred me to set up my own restaurant, Ning, in Manchester back in 2006. Here the menu is filled with classics like *Roti Canai* (page 28) and *Rendang* (page 96) as well as more unusual dishes like Spicy Baked Haddock (page 65) where I take traditional flavours less commonly seen in the UK and work them up into delicious dishes using local seasonal ingredients. But still I miss the delicious street-food snacks like Char Kuey Teow fried noodles (page 146) that you find on every street corner in Penang.

This book is like a love letter to everything that is great about Malaysian cooking. From well-known classics and simple street food to special festive dishes, it is full of recipes which mean so much to me, and taste so good that I had to share them.

Food is at the heart of Malaysian life. Big cook-ups for family gatherings, eating street food at roadside hawker stalls, and cooking banquets for 2,000 guests are all part of our cultural scene. What's more, eating is a 24/7 activity, and it's certainly not unheard of for us to eat out at 2 a.m., with the whole family in tow.

Although there are now supermarkets chains in most cities, traditional street food is alive and kicking up and down the country. Out on the streets you'll find the full-on sensory experience of real Malaysian food: from village markets touting a kaleidoscopic array of fruits and vegetables, to curb-side stalls offering one single, exquisite dish. So in this book I have devoted the first chapter to street food and the last chapter to Malaysian kitchen essentials. These chapters will give you the tools to cook like a true and passionate Malaysian cook, just like my mum who taught me how to do it all.

Diversity

Food is what brings us Malaysians together, and we are rightly proud of it. Our food has an incredibly rich blend of influences. Think Portuguese-meets-Arab-meets-Indian-meets-Chinese-meets-Thai-and-Indonesian and you're getting close! Admittedly you don't find all these flavours in one single recipe, as different dishes combine different influences. But the point is that Malaysia has a complex ethnic history and this makes for amazing food.

There are three major ethnic groups in Malaysia: native Malay, Chinese and Indian. And Malaysia has also been colonized in the past by the Portuguese, Dutch and British. All these have left a significant mark. Nutmeg, for example, was originally planted by the British in Penang Island and today this is still the big attraction of this area where I grew up.

Malaysian food has also been influenced by its neighbouring countries. In the north our food tends to have a Thai influence whereas in the South the food is more Javanese. Our love of curry is a hand-me-down from countries further afield like Sri Lanka and India.

I am Malay, and this is the biggest ethnic community in Malaysia. There is lots of regional variation to Malay tastes. In the north we like our dishes spicier thanks to the Thai influence. In the South there's a more fragrant Indonesian mood. Typical Malay food includes meat curries like *rendang* (page 96) and seafood curries like *gulai* (page 63). Turmeric and coconut milk are much loved ingredients such as in *masak lemak* (page 106).

Chinese Malaysian is the second biggest ethnicity. Chinese flavours come from the early immigrants from southern China who came to work in the tin mines. Traditional Chinese dishes have gradually evolved to suit Malaysian tastes and use local ingredients. Typical Chinese Malaysian food includes noodles as *char kuey teow* (page 146), soups like *bak kut teh* (page 88) and rice dishes like Hainanese chicken rice (page 152), all of which share characteristic flavours of garlic, ginger and oyster sauce. I grew up in Penang, which is predominantly Chinese so I learnt about Chinese flavours from a young age.

The third largest community in Malaysia is Indian. Their ancestors first came from Tamil Nadu in the South and Sri Lanka to work on the rubber plantations. Malaysian Indian dishes now use local ingredients but still feel authentic with their spicy sauces. Lamb curry is a popular Indian Malaysian dish (page 92), as is fish curry (page 56) but not beef, since the cow is considered sacred. As in South India, vegetarian dishes using lentils and spices are popular, like *masalodeh* (page 42) and *dhal* curry (page 126).

As well as these major influences there are many other smaller communities who are known for their own delicious contributions to Malaysia's diverse food scene. The Muslim Mamak community's signature recipe is *roti canai* (page 26) – and it's Mamak food I crave whenever I return to Malaysia. The Nyonya people's heritage is Chinese and one classic Nyonya dish in this book is Kapitan Curry (page 95).

Other groups in Malaysia include indigenous tribes who traditionally use ingredients foraged from the forest like bamboo shoots; people with Afghan and Pakistani heritage whose cooking has a Middle Eastern twist; and Portuguese-Eurasians whose recipes recall European food but with a distinctly Malaysian flavour – think Devil's curry (page 105).

As a chef, I have been lucky enough to learn about all sorts of Malaysian cooking beyond the Malay-style cooking I grew up with. I draw on all these sources in my cooking and I am proud of the diversity of Malaysian food. I am currently acting as Kuala Lumpur's 'Food Ambassador' to promote our unsung cuisines to the rest of the world, which has been a wonderful experience.

Hospitality

'Dah makan?' 'Have you eaten?' That's the question your Malaysian host will ask when you visit. Expect an abundance of food – at the very least they will offer drinks and nibbles. They will be embarrassed if they have nothing to serve you, and a proud host will insist you stay and join them for a meal. Once when I was ill as a kid and missed a couple of days of school, my friends turned up unannounced to see how I was. My mum made them wait while she fried up noodles for them to eat before they left. They were happy she'd gone to the effort and her cooking made me popular at school.

I once took some British guests on a non-touristy culinary tour of Malaysia. We stopped by the village where my dad grew up, about 20 minutes' drive from where my family live in Butterworth. Surrounded by paddyfields, it has remained untouched. My cousin still lives in the village, but I didn't get round to mentioning to her that we'd be stopping there. When we arrived she was embarrassed to have nothing to offer us. So she and I took my guests to the local grilled seafood restaurant. It was a busy Saturday lunchtime and the place was heaving with people. The owner asked if we had enjoyed the food, and when I told him yes, he couldn't stop smiling. For him, it was an honour for his food to be admired by tourists. The experience was one of the highlights of my culinary tour.

Customs

Traditionally, Malay people ate their meals sitting on the floor, on a mat. Malaysian Indians likewise once sat on the floor to eat. These days modern urban families will sit at a table to eat; and only in villages will people still sit on a mat to eat.

Malays usually eat with their fingers and if someone sharing the meal eats with their fingers it is considered rude not to follow suit. Malaysian Indians also eat with their fingers, from metal trays or sometimes banana leaves. In Chinese households the family meal is eaten at a round table, using chopsticks.

Malaysians don't do courses; the dishes are served all at once. It is the same when eating out, unless the restaurant is catering for tourists. The Chinese love to eat their food piping hot, but Malays are not too bothered about temperature. Most dishes are served cold or lukewarm, though rice has to be warm – a restaurant will receive complaints if it serves cold rice.

We eat at all times of the day in Malaysia - there is such a vast choice available. But we do favour particular dishes at certain times of the day. The typical breakfast for Malays, Chinese and Indians varies. But the most popular breakfast for everyone is *roti canai*. With this flat and flaky bread the dough is stretched into a thin layer and cooked until golden brown. Roti is so moreish and universally loved, people now eat it not just for breakfast but for other meals too.

Rice, the Malaysian staple food, is eaten mainly for lunch. Plain white rice might be served with a fish curry or a vegetable stir-fry. In cities the lunch-hour rush, as in any other city, is between 1 and 2 o'clock, but the curries, stir-fries and vegetables, which are served up in long metal trays, are ready by mid-morning.

Afternoon snacks are eaten between 3 and 5 and light street food is a favourite at this time. A classic teatime snack is prawn fritters (page 36). Little stalls along the streets cater specially to office workers, who have 15 minutes' coffee break before getting back to work and finishing at 5.30.

Dinner is a festive time of day for Malaysians. In the evening, families go out to restaurants, food courts, and popular eateries, like Kampong Bharu in Kuala Lumpur and Gurney Drive in Penang. People love the food courts which have stalls as far as the eye can see. Often the most delicious food will come from the most humble stall, served by a passionate stallholder.

Late-night supper is a big part of how people socialize in Malaysia. Many restaurants and cafés in city centres are open 24 hours a day, and are mostly run by the Mamak, the Indian Muslims. Light snacks like *dosa* and quick noodle stir-fries are some of the classic late-night suppers.

Markets

Malaysian markets are unique. All the different cultures of Malaysia come together in the many wonderful scents and flavours of our markets. The small but lively town of Butterworth where I grew up has a typical market. Divided into different areas, there are Indians selling spices and dried ingredients, Malays selling things like turmeric and halal meat, and Chinese selling seafood and vegetables like pak choi.

When I was younger we lived in a block of flats and shared a floor with four Malay families, four Chinese families and two Indian families. You can imagine the different recipes and flavours that we swapped batches of notes on.

My neighbour, Ah Lian, was Chinese and she and her husband were fishmongers at the local market, so we would be inundated with fish.

I loved the way food brought us all together. During the festive seasons we would always exchange traditionally baked cookies.

In Kuala Lumpur, my favourite is Chow Kit market. It's always so busy and full of life, and whenever I go there I immediately feel part of it, no matter how long I have been away. There are people bartering for the best fresh produce, others sampling the freshly picked fruit, and it is bursting at the seams with typically Malaysian street food stalls. Other great markets to look out for are Pudu market, a classic fresh market that opens in the mornings near Jalan Pasar, and Kampong Bahru Pasar Minggu, a Sunday market in Kuala Lumpur.

Malaysia is also famous for its night markets, which I remember being introduced in the mid-1980s. A typical night market starts around 5.30 p.m. and finishes at about 10.30. Back then, if you worked, there was little alternative for you to get a good chance to shop. I remember everyone in the village where I lived was so excited when the night market first opened – not only were we able to buy food but there were also stalls selling clothes, household and electrical goods at affordable prices. The markets gave families a chance to get together, dine out and bond over great food.

Malaysian food stalls are quite different from others I have seen around the world, as they tend to concentrate on just a few dishes but make those great. Some places sell only one dish, but it will taste amazing because so much love has gone into it. I always say, whatever you do in life make sure you are passionate about it. For example, we used to drive an extra half an hour or more to find the best satay stall. To this day, when I go back to Malaysia my brother will still do the drive to get us a mountain of sumptuous chicken satay skewers.

Cooking with my mum

I owe a lot of thanks to my late mum for passing on her cooking skills to me. Because I was so persistent, always wanting to help cook, I became her 'favourite' kitchen assistant. In Malaysian culture the daughter is traditionally expected to help in the kitchen, not the son. But somehow that perception changed in our neighbourhood – my mum's friends knew that I was like another 'daughter' when it came to cooking. My elder sister wasn't interested, and spent most of her time watching TV with my younger brother.

My mum was passionate about what she did, and particular about how she did it. Cooking with my mum was quite a challenge at times. She was a perfectionist and expected her food to be not just good but excellent.

When I was young my parents had a stall in the morning market and another in the night market. In the morning they would sell freshly made *nasi lemak* or coconut rice (page 153) and in the night market they sold *mee rebus* or noodles in broth (page 170). In the early '90s my parents took over the local council office's canteen and their daily routine began with a visit to the market at 4 a.m. each day. I followed them once and was amazed that they'd do that every single day. The local market traders knew my mum well and she was always their priority customer. She was so picky about the ingredients she bought; they had to be truly fresh. My dad would always wait in the car, minding his own business and reading the newspapers with sweet tea (page 196).

The pace in mum's canteen was on another level to her kitchen at home: stressful, tense and fast. She had eighteen staff and served breakfast, brunch, lunch and tea. For breakfast she cooked *nasi lemak* (page 153), fried noodles and fritters. Brunch was something light but lunch, however, was like a festival of dishes. For tea she fried noodles, made porridge and fritters, like *cucur badak*, sweet potato patties. The canteen was busy all the time – I think some of her customers were just visitors who'd heard about the great food. Every meal had to be ready on time and she was really quick in the kitchen. She disliked any lazy staff – well, who doesn't – and if they were not committed she asked them to leave.

She also took any customer complaint deadly seriously, but only with regard to quality, not price. If a customer asked for a cheaper price, she tell them to take a hike. I'm not sure she's the best role model for customer service, but her customers were all extremely loyal.

Mum would delegate her staff to prepare the ingredients but she did most of the cooking herself. For lunch alone, there were more than twenty dishes. She cooked a few dishes at a time – with the four gas burners all on the go. The woks were huge, and so were the pots for the curries. On weekdays, she cooked for a few hundred customers, but the busiest day and the highlight of the week was Saturday, with more than 1,000 people. Back then Malaysians worked half day on Saturday and finished at lunchtime, and workers from nearby offices came to the canteen to enjoy the tomato rice (page 145), *ayam masak merah* (page 103), *daging masak kicap* (page 100) and *dhal* curry (page 126). A simple menu but loved by all her customers.

She would start her curries by frying the shallots, garlic and ginger - beautifully sliced by her staff - in oil. She used dried chillies a lot in her cooking, soaked and puréed. She added spices and curry leaves to some of her curries and pandan leaves to others. Her tips for cooking beautiful curries was to wait till the aroma rises and the herbs and spices are golden brown. This method, called *tumis* in Malaysia, is like an Asian twist on the European sofrito or mirepoix. Next Mum added curry paste, tamarind and thick coconut milk and simmered it until the oil separated - to make a good curry it's important the curry paste cooks properly. Next she added meat to one pot and fish to the other. Vegetables like tomato or okra were added at the end.

The canteen kitchen was boiling hot, with just one fan. I couldn't spend long in there, and mum wasn't keen to have me there either. Most of her staff were female. Male staff were out the front with my dad, who sat at the cashier's table and did the takings. He always had a small white towel wrapped around his forehead to stop him sweating. When he had that towel on, we knew he meant business.

My parents' glory years running the council's canteen were one of the best things that happened to them. Even now customers will reminisce to me on Facebook about my mum's cooking. They are much missed.

Mum at Ning

My parents came to visit me in Manchester in 2006, a few months before I was due to open Ning. I had already planned to open the restaurant but didn't have the courage to tell them while they were here, as I knew they would oppose the idea. Sadly my dad passed away in Malaysia two weeks after their visit, which was heartbreaking for my mum, as they were never apart. To help with her grief, I invited her back to the UK to spend time with me. She agreed, and came over three weeks after I opened Ning, in December 2006. I told her about the restaurant only a few days before she was due to travel. Her reaction made me rather nervous, and at that point I never dreamed she would take over my kitchen.

She arrived in winter, and her first remark was, 'It's too cold and I can feel it in my stomach!' I laughed when she said that. I had to put a heater on full power in her bedroom. The day after she arrived, I took her to the restaurant and introduced her to my staff. When it first opened the restaurant wasn't as busy as it is now. I bought her a comfortable chair so she could take a nap in the office when she felt tired, as she was reluctant to rest at home. The chair was no use, as she spent most of her time in the kitchen. She gave my staff instructions and even cooked some of the dishes herself. My staff did what she told them. Whenever she needed a break, she went out front and sat at the Table 1, close to the bar, the 'VIP table' where I sat friends who came to dine at Ning, so I could easily pop out and greet them. One customer said how nice it was to see the chef come out and watch the diners enjoying her food. My mum giggled when I told her the customers thought she was the head chef.

She took control in the kitchen and told me and my staff what to do. She suggested desserts to include on the menu, one of which was banana fritter balls. My chefs learnt a lot from her, but I had to translate for the non-Malay-speaking ones, as she didn't speak English. The only word she knew was 'Good!' and at the same time she would put her thumb up when she asked the customers whether her food was good or not.

Having Mum in my kitchen inspired us all greatly. My staff saw what it means to be a truly passionate cook. Nemesia, who has been with Ning from day one, still talks about her, which can bring me to tears thinking about the time when she was here. The dishes on my menu were mostly inspired by what she used to cook and became bestsellers, like *daging masak kicap* (beef in soy sauce, page 100) and *ikan goreng masam manis* (fillets of seabass in sweet and sour sauce, page 59). Without her inspiration, I wouldn't have made Ning the success it is today. And if you cook the recipes in this book you are helping her legacy carry on. Thank you.

ABANG LONG CO...
D'ALO...

NASI CAMPUR	SUP/TOM YAM	NASI GORE...
LAUK-PAUK	-EKOR	-BIASA
-AYAM MERAH	-AYAM	AYAM
-AYAM KUNYIT	-DAGING	-KAMPU...
-SIPUT	-TULANG	-CINA
-UDANG	-SEAFOOD	-PAPRIK
-SOTONG	-CENDAWAN	-DAGING
	-MAGGIE	-PATAYA

Street Food
& Snacks

Chicken Satay Skewers SATE AYAM

4 stalks of lemongrass (use bottom
  half only)
1kg boneless chicken thighs, cut into
  10cm-long strips
3 tablespoons ground turmeric
½ tablespoon ground cumin
2 teaspoons fine sea salt
3 tablespoons white sugar
30 bamboo satay skewers, 17.5cm
  long (soaked in water for 30 minutes
  if barbecuing)

For the brushing oil
100ml vegetable oil
1 tablespoon white sugar
50ml coconut milk
1 stalk of lemongrass, bruised

For the garnish
1 red onion, cut into thick slices
1 cucumber, cut into small wedges

Makes 30

Chicken satay is always a crowd-pleaser and is an ideal party dish. There are many different types of marinade, and this is one of the simplest, giving the chicken a smoky caramelized flavour with a hint of lemongrass, cumin and turmeric. For a complete satay meal, it is served with peanut sauce, cucumber wedges, red onion slices and, if you want to be really authentic, cubes of pressed rice.

----

1 Blitz the lemongrass with a dash of water until smooth, using a food processor or hand blender. Transfer to a bowl and add the chicken, turmeric, cumin, salt and 3 tablespoons of sugar. Mix thoroughly, then leave to marinate for at least 2 hours, and preferably overnight in the refrigerator.

2 Carefully thread the chicken pieces on to the bamboo skewers. The meat should cover the skewer to prevent it getting burnt when grilling. Cover the tip of the skewer too. To make the brushing oil, put the oil, sugar and coconut milk into a small bowl and mix well.

3 Satay is best when cooked on a barbecue or a charcoal grill; alternatively you can use a griddle pan. Place the chicken skewers on the barbecue or grill and use the bruised lemongrass to coat them with the oil mixture and keep the moisture in. Turn the skewers to make sure the chicken is cooked evenly.

4 When the chicken is cooked through, and is brown and slightly charred, garnish with the onion and cucumber and serve with peanut sauce (see page 220).

Malay Net Pancake ROTI JALA

I've lost count of how many cookery class students I've shown how to make this. It's made from basic pancake ingredients with two additions: turmeric and coconut milk. These turn it into a savoury dish, best served with a curry. From what I've seen, children are better at making this than adults. The full concentration they give to it puts adults to shame! The traditional *roti jala* pourer has five long nozzles, but you can create a makeshift one yourself by carefully punching five holes in the bottom of the used coconut milk tin, or by using a piping bag.

400g plain flour
1 egg
200ml coconut milk
½ tablespoon ground turmeric
1 teaspoon fine sea salt
4 tablespoons vegetable oil
1 pandan leaf, tied into a knot (or
  1 stalk of bruised lemongrass)

Makes 20–25

----

1 Put the flour, egg, coconut milk, turmeric and salt into a bowl. Add 725ml of water, mix well, then blend until the mixture becomes a smooth batter that will coat the back of a ladle.

2 Place a flat pan on a medium heat, and glaze the pan with a touch of oil, using the pandan leaf, which will give a scented aroma to the batter.

3 Put a roti jala pourer (see above) on to a bowl or a deep plate to avoid dripping. Scoop up some of the batter with the ladle, drop it into the pourer, and bring it to the pan. Using the pourer, make circles of batter starting from the middle of the pan. Continue moving outwards, with the circles overlapping, keeping the flow of batter constant, until you have a pancake around 20cm in diameter. It will look like a net – you can use your own creativity here. The pourer should be held approximately 6cm above the pan for the best results.

4 Cook for half a minute, until the pancake can be easily lifted around the edge with a palette knife or pan slice. Transfer it on to a work surface, then fold the sides inwards and roll it from bottom to top. Repeat until all the batter is used up.

5 Serve with simple Malay chicken curry (see page 85).

Malaysian Flatbread ROTI CANAI

This famous Mamak dish is considered 'sacred', as most of the people who know how to make it are not willing to share the recipe. I asked for it many times, but no one would tell me! At last I've managed to find it, and I've perfected it by adding coconut water to improve its crispy flakiness. You can use coconut water or you can just use water if you like. The ingredients are inexpensive, but the technique is a little tricky at first. Once you've practised, I can guarantee you will be an expert, like a Mamak in Malaysia. A good flatbread should be flaky on the outside and soft inside – to achieve this, you need to puff it like a pillow with both palms of your hands as soon as you've cooked it to a crispy brown.

These flatbreads are best served with a fish curry, in my opinion, but most Malaysian food stalls serve them with vegetable *dhal*.

600g plain flour, plus a little extra
  for kneading
1½ teaspoons fine sea salt
100ml coconut water
1 egg
2 tablespoons vegetable oil,
  plus 750ml vegetable oil for
  the marinade
4 tablespoons condensed milk

Makes 10

1 Put the flour and salt into a large bowl and mix thoroughly.

2 Put the coconut water, egg, 2 tablespoons of oil and condensed milk into a medium bowl or measuring jug, then add 170ml of water and stir well. Add this mixture to the bowl of flour and knead for 10 minutes until smooth and elastic.

3 Cover the bowl with clingfilm and leave to prove for 30 minutes. Add a little flour to the dough and knead again, then leave to prove for another 30 minutes. Knead again, then divide the dough into 10 dough balls about the size of a small fist. When dividing the dough, use your thumb and index finger to squeeze and cut the dough. The technique is to make sure there is no join in the dough ball, so the dough can be stretched into one thin piece. Put the dough balls into a deep plate, then pour 750ml of oil over until it covers all the balls. Leave to marinate for a minimum of 4 hours, or overnight.

4 Put one of the dough balls on an oiled work surface and use your palm to stretch and flatten it, then flip and stretch it a few times more so that it becomes thinner and larger. Fold the sides, top and bottom over, to get a square shape with air trapped in between the layers.

5 Heat a little oil in a flat pan and fry the dough until both surfaces are golden brown and have a crisp texture. Now place the fried flatbread on a clean surface and puff it up from the edge inwards so it crumples. Repeat with the rest of the dough, and serve with curry, for dipping.

Beef Murtabak (Omelette Wrapped in Roti)

MURTABAK DAGING

For the wrapping
1 × Malaysian flatbread dough (see page 28), divided into 10 pieces, or 20 ready-made (30 × 30cm) spring roll wrappers

For the filling
2 tablespoons vegetable oil
2½ large onions, diced
2 cloves of garlic, finely chopped
2.5cm fresh ginger, finely chopped
3 tablespoons ground spice mix for meat (see page 211), mixed with a dash of water
½ teaspoon fine sea salt
1 tablespoon tamarind paste (or lemon or lime juice)
300g minced beef
200g potatoes, boiled for 10 minutes with skins on, then peeled and mashed
6 eggs
Vegetable oil for shallow frying

Makes 10

This dish is actually *roti canai* (Malaysian flatbread, see page 28) with a filling. That is the best way of describing it. The filling can be of minced beef, chicken or lamb, with diced onion, potato, spices and eggs, but you can make it as a vegetarian dish too. It is traditionally served with a curry sauce and sliced pickled onions. *Murtabak* is very popular at Malaysian night markets, and there is one stall not far from my friend's place near Bangi in Selangor that sells an especially good one. It's the best I ever tried, and it was very good value for money, like all street food in Malaysia.

----

1 Heat a large frying pan over a medium heat. Add the oil and cook the onions for 2 minutes, then add the garlic and ginger and continue frying for 1 minute.

2 Add the spice mix, salt and tamarind paste and cook until the sauce has thickened. Add the beef and fry for 3 minutes, until cooked through. Add the mashed potato, stir well and cook for 2 minutes, then turn the heat off.

3 Break the eggs into a large bowl and beat gently. Add the cooked mixture and mix thoroughly. There is no need to wait until the filling cools down completely before mixing it with the eggs – the heat will cook the eggs slightly and thicken the filling.

4 Stretch out one of the pieces of dough on a flat surface, then place it on a round plate and add 3 tablespoons of filling. Make sure the stretched dough has no holes, otherwise the filling will leak out. Wrap it, side to side, to make a square parcel. Repeat with the rest of the dough and filling.

5 Heat a frying pan with a little oil over a low heat. Once the oil is hot, gently flip the wrapped parcels off the plate and into the frying pan, a few at a time, making sure the pastry does not tear, otherwise the filling will come out. Fry for 2–3 minutes on each side, until golden brown. Gently press with a spatula to check – if the *murtabak* are still soft, they are not cooked. Repeat with the rest of the *murtabak*, using a little more oil each time.

6 Serve with onion relish (see page 224) and curry sauce (page 219).

Crunchy Fried Spring Rolls

POPIAH GORENG

You can't beat classic spring rolls for a party or as an appetizer. But don't put up with cheap, tasteless frozen ones from the supermarket – make your own, fresh. I love to pack mine with crunchy vegetables, and serve them with a sweet chilli dip. My favourite root vegetable to use is jicama, as it gives a sweet and crunchy texture to the rolls. If you can't find it, you can use extra carrot, mooli, white radish or daikon instead, but soak them in ice-cold water for 15 minutes to make them crunchy. You can add prawns if you like, to make the rolls even more special. You can make the wrappers yourself (see page 216) or simply buy them ready-made from the supermarket.

----

1 Heat 1 tablespoon of oil in a wok or a large frying pan over a high heat and cook the garlic until golden brown. Add the beansprouts, jicama, carrot, oyster or mushroom sauce and salt and fry for 2 minutes, until the vegetables wilt slightly. Turn off the heat, then scoop out into a colander and drain for 5 minutes. This prevents the wrappers from soaking up the moisture and going soggy.

2 Place one of the wrappers on a flat surface with the corners pointing upwards and downwards into a diamond shape, and spoon on a tablespoon of the filling, starting at the bottom corner. Roll the wrapper over the filling, gently squeeze to make a tight roll, then continue to roll halfway up. Fold the left and right sides inwards, roll up to the top, then brush with a little water to seal. Repeat with the remaining wrappers and filling.

3 Heat the oil for frying in a saucepan over a medium heat. To check whether the oil is hot enough, dip the end of a wooden spoon into the oil – it will bubble around the spoon when it's ready for frying, and should measure between 180°C and 200°C on a kitchen thermometer. Fry the spring rolls for 4–5 minutes, until golden brown and crisp, then scoop out with a slotted spoon and drain on kitchen paper. If your saucepan is small, fry them in batches.

4 Arrange the spring rolls next to each other on a serving dish, then brush the *sambal* on top and sprinkle with the fried shallots, if you like. Serve straight away.

1 tablespoon vegetable oil, plus 500ml vegetable oil for shallow frying
3 cloves of garlic, finely chopped
100g beansprouts
300g jicama (or alternatives, see left), julienned
1 medium carrot, julienned
2 tablespoons oyster or mushroom sauce
A pinch of fine sea salt
20–25 ready-made spring roll wrappers (30 × 30cm)
sweet chilli sambal (see page 217)
4 tablespoons ready-made fried shallots, for garnish (optional)

Makes 20–25

Soft Spring Rolls POPIAH BASAH

20–25 spring roll wrappers (see page 216, or use ready-made wrappers)
sweet chilli sambal (see page 217)

For the filling
2 tablespoons vegetable oil
1 medium onion, thinly sliced
4 cloves of garlic, finely chopped
30g dried shrimps, soaked in warm water for 5 minutes (optional)
250g jicama, peeled and shredded using a grater
200g beansprouts
100g carrots, peeled and shredded using a grater
3 tablespoons oyster sauce
1 teaspoon fine sea salt
½ teaspoon ground white pepper

For the garnish
4 tablespoons crushed roasted peanuts
6 pieces of ready-made fried spongy tofu, finely chopped
A 1-egg omelette, cut into strips
4 tablespoons ready-made fried shallots

Makes 20–25

Traditional Malaysian spring rolls (*popiah*) are not deep-fried, but are made with a soft spring roll pastry that has been lightly cooked in a frying pan (see page 216 if you want to learn how to do this). I guess it's our version of a tortilla. Simple, tasty hand-held street food – but requiring the skill of an expert. There's an old gentleman in his seventies by Chowrasta market in Georgetown, Penang, who still does this every day. But it's a dying art – sadly, as *popiah* are much tastier and more rustic when handmade rather than factory-made. However, with my step-by-step guide you can become an expert too, and we can all keep the tradition alive. If you can't find jicama, you can use extra carrot, mooli, white radish or daikon instead, soaked in ice-cold water for 15 minutes.

----

1 To make the filling, heat the oil in a wok or a large frying pan over a medium heat and cook the onion and garlic until fragrant and golden brown. Add the dried shrimps (if using) and cook for 1 minute, then add the jicama, beansprouts, carrots, oyster or mushroom sauce and salt. Cook for 2 minutes, until the vegetables wilt, then turn off the heat. Add the white pepper, give it a stir, then scoop out into a colander and set aside for 3–4 minutes to drain the juice (there is no need to drain completely, as the spring rolls are served soft and moist).

2 Place one of the spring roll wrappers on a flat surface and spoon on 1 tablespoon of the filling, starting at the bottom corner. Roll the wrapper over the filling, gently squeeze to make a tight roll, then continue to roll halfway up. Fold the left and right sides inwards and roll up to the top, then brush with a little water to seal. Repeat with the remaining wrappers and filling.

3 Arrange the spring rolls next to each other on a platter or large plate and brush the sambal on top. Garnish with crushed peanuts, crispy tofu, omelette strips and fried shallots and serve immediately.

Prawn Fritters CUCUR UDANG

125g plain flour
25g self-raising flour
1½ teaspoons ground turmeric
1½ teaspoons fine sea salt
750ml vegetable oil, for frying
200g beansprouts
100g Chinese garlic chives (or spring
  onions), cut 2.5cm long
12 raw king prawns, peeled

Serves 2–3

My favourite *cucur udang* stall is in Georgetown, next to Chowrasta Market. Three generations of the same family have run the stall, and I remember going there with my family every time we went to Penang Island for a shopping trip.

My recipe is slightly different from the one served at the stall. I use king prawns, and a lot of garlic chives and beansprouts to give the fritters extra crunchiness. To make the batter crispy I add self-raising flour, but you could also use rice flour. If you can't find garlic chives, use chopped spring onions instead.

These fritters are best served with peanut sauce, but they are sometimes served with a sweet chilli sauce too. They are popular with my restaurant guests, and make a lovely filling snack at any time of the day.

----

1 Put the plain and self-raising flours, turmeric and salt into a bowl and add 500ml of water, bit by bit, giving it a good stir until the mixture becomes a smooth and thick batter.

2 Heat a wok or a deep saucepan over a medium heat. Add the oil and test it with a piece of beansprout to check if the oil is hot enough. If it sizzles, it's ready. If you have a thermometer, the temperature should be between 180°C and 200°C.

3 Add the beansprouts, chives and prawns to the batter and fold in with a spoon to create a small ball, one prawn per ball. Gently drop each batter ball into the oil. Avoid making the balls too big, as they will take longer to cook and may burn outside but not be fully cooked inside. Fry in batches if necessary.

4 Fry each ball for 2–3 minutes, until crispy and golden brown, then scoop out with a slotted spoon and serve with peanut or chilli sauce (see pages 220 and 206).

Crispy Beancurd Rolls with Chicken

LOH KEI BAK

This is a popular street food on Chinese stalls. The rolls are normally deep-fried, but in my recipe I shallow-fry them, using less oil. It gives the same result, and the fact is, everything else is cooked, it just gives a crunchy texture to the beancurd skin. If you can't find beancurd skins, you can use wonton or spring roll wrappers. Jicama is a type of root that looks similar to yam, but with a juicier and crunchier texture. It can be eaten fresh. If you can't find jicama, use extra carrot, mooli, white radish or daikon, but soak them in ice-cold water for 15 minutes to make them crunchy. Serve with dark chilli sauce.

----

1 To make the filling, heat a large frying pan over a medium heat, add the tablespoon of oil and sauté the garlic for a few seconds, until fragrant. Add the chicken, five-spice and white pepper and cook until the chicken pieces are sealed. Add the jicama, carrot, light soy sauce, sesame oil and salt, and cook until the vegetables are well mixed and slightly wilted. Add the egg and gently stir until the filling thickens. Finally add the spring onion. Give a good stir and turn the heat off.

2 Place a piece of beancurd skin on a work surface and place 2 tablespoons of filling in the middle. Start wrapping from the bottom and gently roll to the middle, then fold in the sides and continue rolling to the top. Brush with the cornflour paste to seal the roll. Repeat with the remaining beancurd skin and filling.

3 Heat the oil for frying in a medium frying pan over a low heat. You will probably need to fry the rolls in two or three batches. Once the oil is ready, lower the rolls gently into the oil and fry for 2–3 minutes, until crispy brown. Take out, using a slotted spoon, and dab with kitchen paper to remove excess oil.

4 Serve straight away, with dark chilli sauce or chilli and vinegar dip (see pages 206 and 207).

10 squares of beancurd skin
 (20 × 20cm)
1 tablespoon cornflour, mixed with
 a dash of water to make a paste
250ml vegetable oil for shallow
 frying

For the filling
1 tablespoon vegetable oil
4 cloves of garlic, finely chopped
300g chicken, minced
2 teaspoons ground five-spice,
 mixed with a dash of water
½ teaspoon ground white pepper
200g jicama (or alternatives,
 see left), shredded
1 carrot, shredded
1 tablespoon light soy sauce
½ teaspoon sesame oil
½ teaspoon fine sea salt
1 egg, beaten
1 spring onion, cut into 0.5cm slices

Makes 10

Grilled Sticky Rice PULUT UDANG

8 pieces of banana leaf
  (or aluminium foil), 18 × 18cm
300g sticky rice, soaked in water
  for 4 hours or overnight
100ml coconut milk
1½ teaspoons fine sea salt
3 tablespoons vegetable oil
1 teaspoon ground cumin
1 teaspoon ground turmeric
1 teaspoon fine sea salt
1 teaspoon white sugar
20g dried shrimps, soaked in warm
  water for 10 minutes (or fresh
  prawns)
75g desiccated coconut
1 spring onion, cut into 1cm slices

For the paste
1 shallot
1cm fresh galangal (or ginger)
1 stalk of lemongrass
4 dried chillies, soaked in boiling
  water for 10 minutes

Makes 8 parcels

This dish is sold at street stalls for an afternoon snack, and sometimes at our traditional night markets. On the east coast of Malaysia it is sold with a fish filling and is called *pulut pangyang*. The savoury and aromatic flavour of the turmeric and chilli combines with the nuttiness of the desiccated coconut filling to give a typically Malaysian fusion of sweetness, saltiness and spice. Some people prefer to use fresh prawns instead of the traditional dried shrimps.

----

1 Clean the banana leaves, if using, then soften them by placing them on a low flame or over steam from a kettle for a few seconds.

2 Set up a steamer or put a rack into a wok or deep pan with a lid. Pour in 5cm of water and bring to the boil on a medium heat. Place a deep 23cm round cake tin in the middle of the steamer, then add the sticky rice and steam for 30 minutes.

3 Remove the tin from the steamer and add the coconut milk and salt. Mix well, then steam again for a further 15 minutes. Take the tin out of the steamer and set aside for the rice to cool down.

4 Purée the paste ingredients together until smooth, using a food processor or a hand blender. Heat a wok or a large frying pan over a medium heat, then add the oil and sauté the paste for 2 minutes, until fragrant. Add the cumin, turmeric, salt, sugar and dried shrimps and cook for 1 minute.

5 Add the desiccated coconut and 200ml of water, then turn the heat to low and simmer for 3 minutes, or until the mixture is dry. Finally add the spring onion, stir well and turn off the heat. Transfer the filling to a bowl and leave to cool down completely.

6 Split the sticky rice into 8 portions. Lay a banana leaf (or aluminium foil) flat, scoop on 2 teaspoons of the shrimp filling, then gently wrap around with sticky rice and banana leaf. The technique is like making sushi. Wrap it nice and tight, without tearing the leaf. Use a toothpick to seal the top and bottom of the leaf, then repeat with the rest of the leaves and filling.

7 Grill or dry-fry in a frying pan for 5 minutes on each side.

Minced Beef & Potato Cakes

BEGEDIL DAGING

These potato cakes with minced beef are eaten with clear chicken soup or on their own. To keep the sweetness and starch in for as long as possible before peeling, I recommend that you boil the potatoes with their skins on.

---

1 Bring 3 litres of water to the boil in a large deep saucepan and boil the potatoes for 10–15 minutes, until they are soft. Scoop out with a slotted spoon and rinse with cold water to cool them down slightly. Peel the potatoes and cut them into chunks, then transfer them to a bowl and mash until smooth.

2 Heat a large frying pan over a medium heat. Add the minced beef, cumin and ½ teaspoon of sea salt and cook for 5 minutes, then add to the bowl of mashed potato. Add the spring onions, coriander, white pepper, fried shallots and the remaining salt and mix thoroughly. Shape the mixture into balls 5cm in diameter and gently flatten them on the palm of your hand to make potato cakes 2cm thick.

3 Beat the eggs together in a shallow bowl. Heat a deep medium frying pan over a medium heat and add the oil. To check whether the oil is hot enough, drop in a slice of spring onion and if it starts bubbling, it's ready. Dip the potato cakes into the beaten egg and fry for 2 minutes on each side, until crispy brown. Fry them in batches if you can't fit them all into the pan at the same time.

1kg floury potatoes
250g minced beef
½ tablespoon ground cumin
1½ teaspoons fine sea salt
2 spring onions, cut into 0.5cm slices
4 tablespoons finely chopped fresh
 coriander
1 teaspoon ground white pepper
4 tablespoons ready-made fried
 shallots
4 medium eggs
400ml vegetable oil for frying

Makes 20

Malaysian Indian Lentil Patties

MASALODEH

500g split lentils (chana dhal),
soaked in water for at least 4 hours,
or overnight
2 tablespoons vegetable oil, plus
500ml vegetable oil for frying
2 large onions, diced
4 sprigs of fresh curry leaves (or
6 bay leaves, roughly chopped)
1 tablespoon cumin seeds
1 tablespoon dried chilli flakes
¾ tablespoon fine sea salt
1½ tablespoons white sugar

Makes 20

Heavy on cumin and curry leaves, these delicious Indian patties **are crisp on the outside and soft and floury in the inside. For a good range of different types of Indian patties, you should visit the Brickfields area of Kuala Lumpur. The atmosphere is amazing, especially during the annual Diwali festival. These patties can be eaten either on their own or, if you find them too dry, with a quickly made yoghurt dip. You can try other kinds of lentils, but *chana dhal* is the best – it's available from most Asian shops and supermarket World Food aisles.**

----

1 Drain the lentils, then put them into a food processor and blitz until smooth. Transfer to a large bowl and set aside.

2 Heat a deep medium frying pan over a medium heat and add the 2 tablespoons of oil. When it's hot, cook the onions, curry leaves and cumin until fragrant and the onions are golden brown. Add the mixture to the bowl of lentils. Add the chilli flakes, salt and sugar and mix thoroughly.

3 Gently mould the mixture with your fingers to make 20 round flat patties.

4 Wipe out the frying pan with kitchen paper, then place over a medium heat and add the oil for frying. Fry the patties in batches for 2 minutes on each side, until crisp. Serve immediately, with yoghurt dip (see page 225).

Aromatic Clear Chicken Soup

SUP AYAM

This is a simple-to-make soup which I eat as my comfort food, especially when I am trying to lose weight before flying home to Malaysia. The food temptations there are so irresistible that for a week before I go, I go on a strict diet! I used to do this when I returned there once a year, but now I am making more frequent visits, as I have been appointed as Kuala Lumpur's food ambassador. You might think that I already have such temptations at my restaurant, but it's different when you have other people cooking for you – plus the street food atmosphere in Malaysia is incomparable. This soup is especially good if you have a cold or need something light.

250g baby potatoes, washed
500g chicken pieces, on the bone
1 medium red onion, quartered
100g carrot, thinly sliced
5cm cinnamon stick
2 star anise
4 green cardamom pods
1 teaspoon coarsely ground black pepper
1 teaspoon fine sea salt

Serves 2–3

----

1 Put all the ingredients into a large saucepan with 1.5 litres of water. Bring to the boil, then reduce the heat and simmer, uncovered, for 30 minutes, until the chicken meat falls off the bones.

2 Serve straight away.

Crispy Soft Shell Crabs

KETAM RANGUP

Soft shell crabs are harvested as soon as they have shed their old shells for the new ones, and before their new shells have had time to harden. I once visited a farm in Malaysia and was amazed to see how the crabs were farmed. It is fascinating to learn about the nature and source of your ingredients. If you can't find fresh soft shell crabs, get the frozen type, which are available in oriental supermarkets. They come in different sizes, and my favourite is the jumbo size – the bigger the better, and it's meaty. When fried, the crab becomes crisp and crunchy, and you can eat the whole thing.

150g cornflour
2 teaspoons ground white pepper
2 teaspoons fine sea salt
1½ tablespoons sesame oil
8 soft shell crabs
3 egg whites
500ml vegetable oil, for deep-frying

Serves 3–4

----

1 Put the cornflour, white pepper and salt into a bowl and mix thoroughly. In a separate bowl, gently rub the sesame oil on to the crabs. Dip the crabs into the egg whites, then transfer them to the cornflour mixture and coat them generously. Gently shake to remove excess flour and lay them on a baking tray.

2 Heat a wok or a deep medium frying pan over a medium heat and add the oil. The oil must be hot enough, otherwise the batter will not become crispy. Test it by sprinkling in a bit of the batter – if it sizzles, the oil is hot enough to fry the crabs.

3 Fry the crabs in two or three batches, for 4 minutes per batch or until the batter is brown and crispy. The fewer crabs you fry at once, the less time they will take. Scoop them out with a slotted spoon and serve them straight away. Serve as a starter or snack, with sweet chilli sambal (see page 217).

Grilled Fish Pâté in Banana Leaf

OTAK OTAK

12 pieces of banana leaf
 (or aluminium foil), 20 × 20cm
500g cod fillet, roughly chopped
250ml coconut milk
2 medium eggs, lightly beaten
4 kaffir lime leaves, thinly sliced (or
 strips of rind from 2 limes)
½ teaspoon ground white pepper
½ tablespoon brown sugar
1 teaspoon fine sea salt

For the spice paste
2 shallots
3 cloves of garlic
6–8 dried chillies, soaked in boiling
 water for 10 minutes
5cm fresh galangal (or ginger)
5cm fresh turmeric (or 2 teaspoons
 ground turmeric)
3 stalks of lemongrass (use bottom
 half only)
1 teaspoon shrimp paste, dry-toasted
 (or 2 tablespoons fish sauce)

Serves 4 (makes 12 parcels)

Otak otak **means 'brains' in the Malay language, and the name of this dish is believed to derive from its appearance. The dish is very popular in Johor, to the south of Kuala Lumpur. There are a few different versions, but my favourite is the one wrapped in banana leaves. If you don't have these, you can use aluminium foil.**

----

1 Clean the banana leaves, if using, then soften them by placing them on a low flame or over steam from a kettle for a few seconds. The leaf will turn dark, and will become softer and easy to wrap.

2 Using a food processor or a hand blender, blitz the paste ingredients together until smooth and transfer to a large bowl. Blitz the fish until smooth and add to the paste in the bowl. Add the coconut milk and eggs and mix thoroughly. Add the kaffir lime leaves, white pepper, sugar and salt and give one last good mix.

3 Divide the mixture into 12 portions and place one portion on a piece of banana leaf. Gently wrap the mixture in the leaf, to make a long parcel. Secure both ends with toothpicks by punching them through the leaf. Repeat with the remaining banana leaves and paste.

4 Heat a griddle pan or frying pan over a low heat and cook the parcels for 5 minutes on each side, until the banana leaves have turned brown. Gently press one of the parcels, and if the mixture inside is firm, it is cooked. Serve immediately.

Grilled Tofu TAUHU BAKAR

24 pieces of ready-made fried
 spongy tofu
8 bamboo skewers, 17.5 cm long
½ teaspoon ground white pepper

Serves 4

I discovered this simple way of cooking tofu when I went to visit my friend in Kajang. I never thought something as simple as this could be so delicious. It is all to do with the texture of the tofu: it will not work with the soft, beancurd type of tofu – it needs the pre-fried spongy one, which you can get in packs in most Chinese grocers. After grilling, the crispy outer skin becomes crunchy and really nice to dip in the sauce. It's ideal for a barbecue or to accompany a salad. Alternatively, if you are not using a barbecue, you can simply use a griddle pan. Serve with a sweet chilli sambal or a chilli and vinegar dip.

----

1 Skewer 3 pieces of tofu on each bamboo skewer. Set your griddle pan on a high heat. The pan has to be really hot in order to create a charred effect. Once ready, grill the tofu for 2–3 minutes on each side, in batches if necessary, until charred.

2 Sprinkle with white pepper and serve immediately, with chilli and vinegar dip (see page 207) or sweet chilli sambal (see page 217).

Beef Satay Skewers SATE DAGING

Near the Butterworth Jetty in Penang, where I was brought up, there used to be a food court famous for its satay. It was called Meriam Timbul, which means 'floating cannon', and those who grew up in the area in the 1980s would remember the glory years of Meriam Timbul as the favourite destination for families to stop over after returning from Penang Island via the car ferry. The satay owner was called Leman, and he served a very good beef satay. The skewering technique is important, to prevent the skewers getting burnt. The marinade can also be used for lamb or venison. Serve your satay with a peanut sauce.

----

1 Blitz the lemongrass, galangal and turmeric together with a dash of water until smooth in a food processor or using a hand blender. Transfer to a bowl and add the beef, coriander, cumin, fennel, salt and sugar. Mix thoroughly, then leave to marinate for at least 2 hours, or, better still, overnight in the refrigerator. Carefully thread the pieces of beef on to the bamboo skewers. The meat should cover the skewers, including the tip, to prevent them getting burnt when grilling.

2 To make the brushing oil, put the oil, sugar and coconut milk into a small bowl and mix well.

3 Satay is best when cooked on a barbecue or a charcoal grill; alternatively you can use a griddle pan. Place the beef skewers on a hot grill and use the bruised lemongrass to coat each one with the brushing oil mixture to keep the moisture in. Turn the skewers occasionally to make sure the beef is cooked evenly. Serve with peanut sauce (see page 220).

5 stalks of lemongrass (use bottom half only)
5cm fresh galangal (or ginger)
5cm fresh turmeric (or 2 teaspoons ground turmeric)
1kg beef sirloin, cut into 10cm-long strips
1½ tablespoons coriander seeds, coarsely ground
½ tablespoon ground cumin
½ tablespoon ground fennel
½ teaspoon fine sea salt
3 tablespoons white sugar
30 bamboo satay skewers, 17.5cm long (soaked in water for 30 minutes if barbecuing)

For the brushing oil
100ml vegetable oil
1 tablespoon sugar
50ml coconut milk
1 stalk of lemongrass, bruised at the end

Makes 30 skewers

Kak Besah's Curry Puffs

KARIPAP PUSING KAK BESAH

1 tablespoon black peppercorns
2 teaspoons fennel seeds
1 star anise
5cm cinnamon stick
2 tablespoons vegetable oil, plus
  700ml vegetable oil for frying
2 shallots, finely chopped
2.5cm fresh ginger, finely chopped
500g potatoes, peeled and cut into
  1cm dice
1½ teaspoons fine sea salt
100g raw peeled prawns, roughly
  chopped
2 medium onions, diced
2 tablespoons roughly chopped fresh
  coriander leaves
2 tablespoons spring onions, cut into
  1cm slices

For the pastry
First part (yellow dough)
75g chilled butter, cubed
100g plain flour
Second part (white dough)
250g plain flour
100ml cold water
1 egg, beaten
1 teaspoon fine sea salt

Makes 20

My mum, whose nickname was Kak Besah, was well known for her crispy pastry puffs with potato filling. When I taught my students how to make these as part of my Malaysian masterclass at the restaurant, surprisingly few of them managed to do the crimping as nicely as she did. I wondered if it was my bad teaching, but my sister also took years to learn how to crimp the edges of the pastry properly. This is a very special recipe, as I've always believed that my family survived through selling *karipap*. My dad's salary was not enough to support the whole family, so my mum started a small food stall along the street. She also made this *karipap* for my brother and me to sell at the factories near where we lived, during school term breaks. We were poor, but my parents brought us up well. They showed us how to survive by passing on their cooking skills, but also kept insisting we should get a university degree. In the end, I was the only one in the family to get one, and they were proud enough. Help me to treasure this recipe, as it means a lot to me, and carry on my mum's cooking legacy!

----

1 Dry roast the black peppercorns, fennel, star anise and cinnamon until fragrant. Use a spice grinder or a pestle and mortar to grind or pound the roasted spices until fine. Add 50ml of water to the mixture.

2 Heat a wok or a large frying pan over a medium heat and add the 2 tablespoons of oil. Fry the shallots and ginger until fragrant and golden brown, then add the ground spices and fry for 1 minute. Add the potatoes and salt, stir for another minute, then add 300ml of water – the potatoes should be covered. Simmer over a medium heat until they become soft and dry.

3 Now add the prawns, onions, coriander and spring onions. Cook until the onions soften, then turn off the heat. Set aside and let the potato filling cool down.

4 For the pastry, put the ingredients for the first part (yellow dough) into a bowl and mix until a dough is formed. Set aside. Using a separate bowl, mix together the ingredients for the second part (white dough) until you have a firm dough. Divide each set of dough into 5 round balls. Gently press one of the white dough balls with your fingers until flat, then place a yellow dough ball inside and wrap. Repeat the process to make the remaining dough balls.

5 Sprinkle a little plain flour on a work surface and use a rolling pin to flatten a mixed dough ball, rolling it out to make an oval shape about 1cm thick, then roll from the side to make a long strip. Flatten it again with the rolling pin and roll it again from top to bottom. Using a sharp knife, cut it into four pieces and flatten them again to get oval shapes about 0.5cm thick.

6 Place a spoonful of potato filling on to each oval piece of pastry and fold it in half, pinching the edges to seal. To make a crimped pattern, use your thumb and index finger to pinch and fold around the edges. Repeat with the remaining pastry and filling.

7 Heat the vegetable oil for frying in a large pan over a medium-low heat and fry the karipaps, in batches, until golden brown. Serve warm.

Tofu Stuffed with Crunchy Vegetables

TAUHU SUMBAT

100ml vegetable oil
20 pieces of ready-made fried
 spongy tofu
100g beansprouts
200g cucumber, peeled, deseeded
 and thinly julienned
1 carrot, finely julienned or shredded

Serves 4

Tofu comes in different types and textures. In this recipe, I use the spongy type that has already been fried. You can buy this in packs from most oriental shops, and it is particularly good added to a vegetarian curry. The beancurd variety has quite a bland taste, but the spongy one absorbs flavours, so is good for adding to a curry. In Malaysia, only three types of vegetable are normally used for stuffed tofu – cucumber, beansprouts and the crunchy and sweet jicama – but for this version I have replaced the jicama with carrot, as it is so easy to buy and adds a different colour. Some people prefer to serve this stuffed tofu with chilli sauce, but peanut sauce is my favourite.

----

1 Slit the tofu down one side, cutting halfway through, to create a pocket into which to stuff the vegetables. In a large frying pan, heat the oil over a medium heat and re-fry the tofu, a batch at a time, for 1 minute, until the outer skin becomes crispy. Scoop out and dab with kitchen paper to remove excess oil.

2 Blanch the beansprouts in boiling water for 10 seconds, until slightly wilted. Transfer to a bowl, then add the cucumber and carrot and give everything a good mix.

3 Stuff the tofu with the mixed vegetables, transfer to a platter or large plate, and serve with peanut sauce (see page 220).

Seafood

Aromatic Seafood Curry

KARI MAKANAN LAUT

8 tablespoons vegetable oil
1 star anise
5cm cinnamon stick
2 cloves
2 sprigs of fresh curry leaves, leaves
 picked (or 3 bay leaves)
8 raw king prawns, peeled
250g mussels, in their shells
200–300g squid tubes, scored
100ml coconut milk
1 teaspoon fine sea salt
1 tablespoon lime juice

For the ground spices
1½ tablespoons ground coriander
1 teaspoon ground cumin
1 teaspoon ground fennel

For the paste
3 shallots
5 cloves of garlic
5cm fresh turmeric (or 2 teaspoons
 ground turmeric)
5cm fresh ginger
10 dried chillies, soaked in boiling
 water for 10 minutes
1½ teaspoons shrimp paste, dry-
 toasted (or 2 tablespoons fish
 sauce)

Serves 3–4

When I introduced this in my restaurant as a special spring dish, it quickly became very popular and I decided to add it to our permanent menu. It's a seafood and curry lover's dream. Flavoursome and aromatic, the spices work very well with the seafood, drawing out their juices. I love seafood, so I like to pile the curry up with lots of different shellfish, squid and prawns. If you have a local fishmonger or live near a wholesale market like Billingsgate in London, go there. I'm a great believer in buying the freshest seafood possible and supporting local 'wet' markets, as we call them in Malaysia.

----

1 Blitz the paste ingredients together, with a little water if necessary, in a food processor or using a hand blender, then transfer to a bowl. Add the ground spices and mix thoroughly.

2 In a large saucepan, heat the oil over a medium heat and cook the star anise, cinnamon, cloves and curry leaves until fragrant. Add the paste mix and cook for 2 minutes. Now add the prawns, mussels (discarding any that are open and do not close when tapped) and squid, along with 300ml of water. Cook for 2–3 minutes, until the prawns turn pink, the mussels open and the squid curls up. Discard any mussels that have not opened.

3 Add the coconut milk and salt, give it all a good stir and cook for a further minute. Finally add the lime juice, give it another good stir and turn the heat off. Transfer to a serving dish and serve straight away.

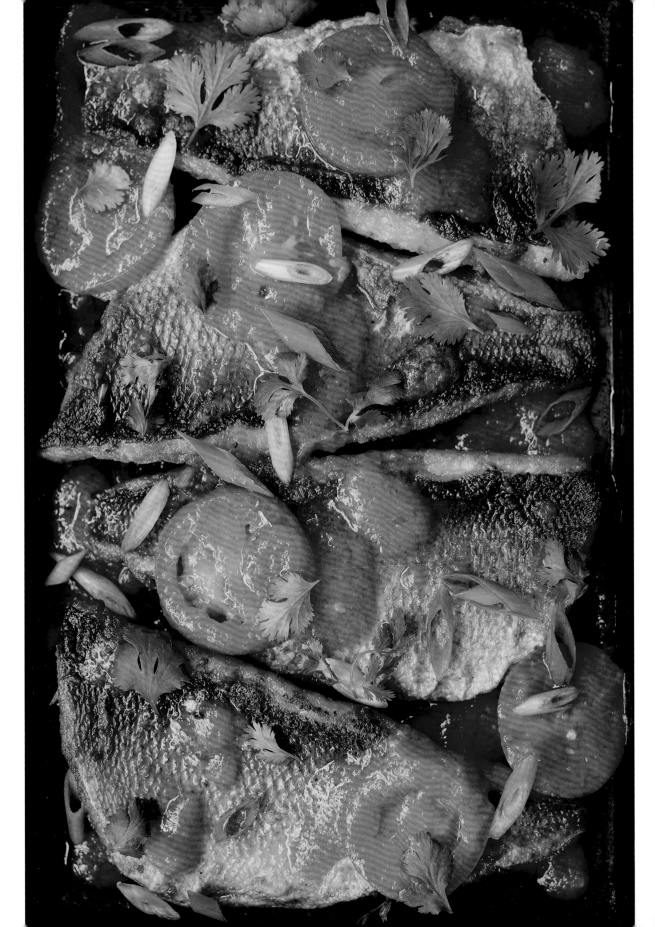

Sea Bass Fillets in Sweet & Sour Sauce

IKAN SIAKAP MASAM MANIS

I once organized my supper club in London around a Malaysian wedding banquet theme, and one of the dishes served was this sweet and sour dish. This special dish is served at the main table at the bride and groom's wedding reception. Traditionally it is made with black pomfret; however, this is difficult to source in the UK, so I use sea bass fillets as an alternative – you want a meaty fish that is able to take on the wonderful flavours.

----

1 Purée the paste ingredients together along with a dash of water until smooth, using a food processor or a hand blender. Rub the turmeric over the fish fillets and sprinkle them with salt.

2 Heat a large frying pan over a medium heat. Add the oil and shallow-fry the fish, two at a time, for 3 minutes on each side, until crisp. Scoop out on to a serving platter and set aside.

3 Use the oil remaining in the pan to sauté the paste for 2 minutes, until fragrant. Add the ketchup, sugar and 1 teaspoon salt, along with 100ml of water, and cook for 1 minute, then add the tomatoes and cook for 1 minute more.

4 Pour the sauce over the fish fillets and garnish with spring onion and coriander. Serve straight away, with jasmine rice.

1 teaspoon ground turmeric
4 sea bass fillets, 150–200g each, cleaned and scored
Fine sea salt
100ml vegetable oil
200ml tomato ketchup
2 tablespoons white sugar
2 medium tomatoes, cut into 1cm slices
1 spring onion, cut into 1cm slices
2 sprigs of fresh coriander, leaves picked

For the paste
1 shallot
2.5cm fresh ginger
5 cloves of garlic
6 fresh red chillies, deseeded

Serves 3–4

Steamed Wild Sea Bass with Lemongrass & Ginger IKAN SIAKAP STIM

4 cloves of garlic
3 bird's-eye chillies
1 teaspoon fine sea salt
1 whole wild sea bass, about
 300–400g, gutted and de-scaled
 (or use sea bass fillets)

For the dressing
1 tablespoon oyster sauce
1 tablespoon fish sauce
3 tablespoons lime juice
½ teaspoon brown sugar
5cm fresh ginger, julienned
2 stalks of lemongrass, thinly sliced
6 kaffir lime leaves (or strips of rind
 from 2 limes)

For the garnish
6 sprigs of fresh coriander, leaves
 picked and roughly chopped
1 red chilli, thinly sliced
1 spring onion, julienned and soaked
 in water for 15 minutes

Serves 3–4

Wild sea bass flesh is firm, with a mild, delicate flavour that works well with this citrus-accented recipe. Other fish that can be used are cod, haddock and pollock. If you like, you can use sea bass fillets rather than a whole fish, and reduce the cooking time to 10 minutes in total rather than 20.

----

1 Pound the garlic and chillies together to a rough paste, using a pestle and mortar. Put the paste into a bowl with the dressing ingredients and 200ml of water and mix thoroughly.

2 Set up a steamer or put a rack into a wok or deep pan with a lid. Pour in 5cm of water and bring to the boil on a high heat.

3 Rub the salt over the fish, then place it in a deep dish or cake tin, place in the steamer, and steam for 10 minutes. Open the lid and pour in the dressing, then put the lid on again and steam for 10–12 minutes, until the fish is cooked through.

4 Garnish with coriander, chilli and spring onion and serve straight away.

Prawn & Spinach Stir-fry

UDANG DAN KANGKUNG GORENG BELACAN

400g spinach (or morning glory
 if you can find it)
1 teaspoon shrimp paste, dry-toasted
 (or 2 tablespoons fish sauce)
5 cloves of garlic
2 tablespoons vegetable oil
1 red chilli, cut into 0.5cm slices
300g raw prawns, peeled
1 tablespoon light soy sauce
3 tablespoons chilli paste, ready-
 made in a jar or homemade (see
 page 204)

Serves 4

Kangkung, also known as water spinach or morning glory, grows wild in Malaysia by riverbanks, ponds and irrigation canals in paddy fields. The stalk is hollow, like a tube, and it is best to split this in half lengthwise so that any dirt can be easily removed. You can make this dish vegetarian by cooking it without the prawns and shrimp paste. I prefer to buy prawns with their tails on – with the high heat they tend to easily overcook or shrink, and leaving the tails on helps prevent this. If you can't find morning glory, use spinach.

----

1 Split the morning glory stalks in half and cut them into pieces about 10cm long. Rinse them with water – there is no need to dry them, as the water remaining on them will help to make the sauce. Mix the shrimp paste with 50ml of water in a small bowl until smooth. Pound the garlic until fine, using a pestle and mortar.

2 In a wok or a large frying pan, heat the oil over a high heat. Add the pounded garlic and the chilli, and sauté until fragrant and golden brown. Add the prawns and soy sauce and cook until the prawns start to turn pink but are not yet fully cooked.

3 Add the chilli paste, the morning glory and the shrimp paste mixture, stir well and cover with a lid. Leave to cook for 2 minutes, then take off the lid and give a good stir. The vegetables should be wilting by now. Give another stir, then turn off the heat and serve straight away.

Prawn Curry with Grilled Pineapple

GULAI UDANG DAN NENAS

I learned to cook when I moved to the UK at the age of twenty to study for a degree in quantity surveying (which is completely irrelevant to what I do now). My cooking talent and knowledge were always there, but I never practised – it was only after I became independent and was living away from my family that I started cooking intensively. With hindsight, I see that I picked up cooking techniques in the UK, but the idea and knowledge came from back home in Malaysia. The adjustment I made to this recipe, one of my late mum's, was grilling the pineapple in order to bring out the intense flavour and caramelize the sugar in the fruit, which added another flavour to the dish. I sincerely hope she would be pleased with this adjustment, even knowing how much she was against my cooking at the beginning of my career. Bless her.

---

1 Mix together the spice mixture ingredients in a bowl along with 100ml of water and set aside.

2 Preheat a griddle pan or a medium frying pan over a high heat and grill the pineapple in two or three batches, for 2 minutes on each side, until it is nicely charred and brown. Set aside.

3 Heat a saucepan over a medium heat. Add the oil, then sauté the onion and garlic until fragrant and golden brown. Add the curry leaves, star anise and cinnamon and cook for 1 minute. Add the spice mixture, tamarind and salt, turn the heat to low and cook for 2 minutes.

4 Now add the prawns, coconut milk and 100ml of water and cook for 2 minutes, or until the prawns have turned pink. Finally add the pineapple and cook for 1 minute more. Serve with jasmine rice.

300g pineapple, roughly cut into chunks
3 tablespoons vegetable oil
1 medium onion, roughly diced
3 cloves of garlic, finely chopped
2 sprigs of curry leaves, leaves picked (or 3 bay leaves)
1 star anise
1 cinnamon
1 tablespoon tamarind paste (or lemon or lime juice)
1 teaspoon fine sea salt
400g raw king prawns, peeled
200ml coconut milk

For the ground spice mixture
1½ tablespoons ground coriander
2 teaspoons ground fennel
1 teaspoon ground cumin
1 teaspoon ground turmeric
2 teaspoons chilli powder

Serves 2–3

Spicy Baked Haddock

IKAN BAKAR BEREMPAH

This recipe comes from descendants of Portuguese colonists in the World Heritage town of Malacca, two hours' drive from Kuala Lumpur. Malacca has a fascinating history, having been ruled by the Portuguese for 300 years from the sixteenth century, then by the Dutch and the British. It's a must-see place for anyone visiting Malaysia. Banana leaves are not edible but are used a lot in Malaysian cooking for wrapping food. Use baking paper if you can't get them. I wrap the leaves in aluminium foil so that the aroma is kept in and infuses the fish. Here I use haddock, but you can use other firm, fleshy fish such as cod or wild sea bass.

----

1 Preheat the oven to 200°C/fan 180 °C/gas mark 6.

2 Clean the banana leaves, if using, then soften them by placing them on a low flame or over steam from a kettle for a few seconds. The leaf will turn dark, becoming softer and easy to wrap.

3 Using a food processor or a hand blender, blitz the paste ingredients together until smooth. Heat the oil in a medium saucepan over a low heat, cook the paste for 4 minutes, then turn the heat off. Put one fish fillet in the centre of each banana leaf and rub it with a quarter of the paste. Place a slice of lemon on each side and sprinkle with the lime leaves and coriander leaves. Fold the banana leaves over, if using, and wrap the fish to make a parcel, then place on a piece of aluminium foil 30 × 30cm and wrap it tightly, with both ends secured. Repeat with the remaining fish fillets.

4 Place on an oven tray and bake for 20 minutes. Serve immediately.

4 pieces of banana leaf, 25 × 25cm (or baking paper)
3 tablespoons vegetable oil
4 haddock fillets, about 200–250g each
2 lemons, cut into 8 slices
4 kaffir lime leaves, thinly sliced (or strips of rind from 2 limes)
4 sprigs of fresh coriander, leaves picked

For the paste
3 shallots
3 cloves of garlic
8 dried chillies, soaked in boiling water for 10 minutes
2 stalks of lemongrass (use bottom half only)
2.5cm fresh galangal (or ginger)
3 macadamia nuts
4 teaspoons ginger flower purée (or lemongrass purée)
1 teaspoon shrimp paste, dry-toasted (or 2 tablespoons fish sauce)
1 teaspoon fine sea salt

Serves 4

Spicy Sour Monkfish Stew

ASAM PEDAS IKAN

3 tablespoons vegetable oil
2 stalks of lemongrass, bruised
1½ tablespoons ginger flower purée
  (or lemongrass purée)
1 teaspoon fine sea salt
1 teaspoon brown sugar
3 tablespoons tamarind paste (or
  lemon or lime juice)
800g monkfish, roughly cut into
  small chunks
10 small okra, both ends trimmed
10 cherry tomatoes
4 sprigs of Vietnamese coriander (or
  mint or Thai basil), leaves picked

For the paste
10 dried chillies, soaked in boiling
  water for 10 minutes
1 medium onion
1 shallot
3 cloves of garlic
5cm fresh turmeric (or 2 teaspoons
  ground turmeric)
2.5cm fresh ginger
½ tablespoon shrimp paste, dry-
  toasted (or 2 tablespoons fish
  sauce)

Serves 4

This dish originates from the state of Negeri Sembilan, and is commonly made with skate. The recipe works well with monkfish, which has a beautiful flavour and texture. Ginger flower gives a fragrance and distinctive flavour to the fish, but use lemongrass if you don't have any – although different, it will still work well. Vietnamese coriander (laksa or daun kesum) can be bought in some oriental supermarkets or from herb growers – if you can't find it, you can use mint or Thai basil leaves.

----

1 Using a food processor or hand blender, blitz the paste ingredients together until smooth.

2 Preheat a saucepan over a medium heat. Add the oil and cook the lemongrass and ginger flower purée until fragrant. Add the paste, then reduce the heat to low and cook for 2 minutes, stirring occasionally.

3 Add the salt, sugar and tamarind and cook for 1 minute. Add the monkfish, okra, tomatoes and Vietnamese coriander. Gently stir the ingredients so that the paste coats and seals the fish. Add 800ml of water, bring to the boil, then turn the heat to low and simmer for 2 minutes, or until the fish is cooked. Serve straight away.

Squid Chilli Sambal SAMBAL SOTONG

4 tablespoons vegetable oil
3 shallots, finely chopped
3 cloves of garlic, finely chopped
2.5cm fresh ginger, finely chopped
6 tablespoons chilli paste, ready-made from a jar or homemade (see page 204)
1 tablespoon brown sugar
½ teaspoon fine sea salt
2 tablespoons tamarind paste (or lemon or lime juice)
1 teaspoon shrimp paste, dry-toasted (or 2 tablespoons fish sauce)
500g squid tubes, cut open, scored criss-cross and cut into pieces
8 cherry tomatoes
1 medium red onion, sliced into thin rings

Serves 4

Squid is best stir-fried over a high heat for a very short time, to avoid a rubbery texture. For this recipe I recommend that the squid is scored and added at the same time as the vegetables, to prevent it getting overcooked. You can buy frozen squid 'tubes' from fishmongers and oriental supermarkets, but feel free to use fresh squid if you prefer. Scoring allows the squid to curl during cooking and absorb other flavours. This recipe gives a good balance of sweet, spicy and sour and is often served with coconut or jasmine rice.

----

1 Heat a wok or a large frying pan over a medium heat. Add the oil and sauté the shallots, garlic and ginger until fragrant and golden brown. Add the chilli paste, sugar, salt, tamarind and shrimp paste, then reduce the heat to low and simmer for 3 minutes, until the oil separates.

2 Add the squid, tomatoes, red onion and 100ml of water and cook for 2 minutes, until the squid has curled up and vegetables have wilted. Turn the mixture on to a platter and serve with jasmine rice or coconut rice (see page 153).

Black Pepper Crab Stir-fry

KETAM GORENG BERLADA

Crabs are delicious in curries or stir-fries. The most well-known stir-fries in Malaysia are the chilli and black pepper crab recipes. For this dish, I used British brown crabs that I bought from Billingsgate, my favourite market. Since I moved down to London from Manchester, it's become my first choice for getting fresh crabs and lobsters. The salted and preserved soya beans can be bought from Chinese grocers.

----

1 If the crabs are still alive, put them into the freezer for 30 minutes to render them comatose, then plunge them into boiling water for about 15 minutes. This is a more humane method than plunging them in fully awake. Once blanched, remove the shells and claws and cut the crabs in half. Keep the claws and discard the shells.

2 Heat a wok or a large deep frying pan over a high heat. Add the oil and sauté the garlic and ginger until golden brown. Add the chilli paste, black pepper, soya beans, soy sauce, oyster sauce, crabs and salt and cook for 2 minutes, until the crabs start to change colour.

3 Pour in the 200ml of boiling water, then cover the wok or frying pan with a lid, turn the heat down to medium and cook for 5 minutes, taking the lid off occasionally to give a good stir. The crabs should be ready and the sauce should have thickened. Scoop out on to a platter and serve.

2 large brown crabs, about 400–500g each
2 tablespoons peanut oil
3 cloves of garlic, finely chopped
1.5cm fresh ginger, finely chopped
1 tablespoon chilli paste, ready-made from a jar or homemade (see page 204)
1 tablespoon black peppercorns, coarsely ground
1 tablespoon salted and preserved soya beans (optional)
1 tablespoon sweet soy sauce
2 tablespoons oyster sauce
½ teaspoon fine sea salt
200ml boiling water

Serves 2

Butter Prawn Stir-fry

UDANG GORENG MENTEGA

1 tablespoon vegetable oil
3 cloves of garlic, finely chopped
1 green chilli, thinly sliced
4 sprigs of curry leaves, leaves
 picked (or 6 bay leaves)
450g raw king prawns, peeled
2 tablespoons evaporated milk
½ teaspoon fine sea salt
½ teaspoon sesame oil

For the egg floss
8 egg yolks
¼ teaspoon fine sea salt
½ teaspoon white sugar
150g unsalted butter, melted
¼ teaspoon ground white pepper

Serves 2–3

Some friends once took me to a restaurant called Nong & Jimmy, in the heart of Kuala Lumpur, known for its amazing seafood dishes and owned by a Thai and Malaysian couple. The first dish I tried was a butter prawn stir-fry – it was beautifully cooked and tasted awesome. The dish has to be cooked on a high heat to get the egg floss crispy so it melts in your mouth.

----

1 To prepare the egg floss, whisk the egg yolks, salt and sugar together in a bowl. Heat a wok or a deep medium frying pan over a high heat. Add the butter, then pour in the egg slowly, at the same time continuously stirring to create the floss. When the eggs hit the butter stir them around. This will stop the eggs clumping up together and they will form strands of egg floss. Continue stirring until the egg floss turns golden brown. Scoop out and strain off the excess butter. Sprinkle with sugar, sea salt and white pepper and give it a good mix. Set aside.

2 Put the wok or frying pan back on a medium heat. Add the oil and stir-fry the garlic, chilli and curry leaves for a few seconds. Immediately add the prawns, evaporated milk and salt and stir-fry for 2 minutes, until the prawns turn pink and are cooked. Add the sesame oil and give it all a good stir, then transfer to a platter. Top the prawns with the egg floss and serve straight away.

Traditional Fish Curry

KARI IKAN ASLI

This curry is influenced by the cooking of southern India, which was brought to Malaysia by Indian immigrants working in the rubber plantations over 100 years ago. However, the influence of Indian cooking in general can be traced back earlier, to Indian traders. Most households and eateries in Malaysia cook everyday curries using a ready-made curry powder. It is rare to find curries that are cooked from scratch, like this traditional *kari ikan*. I make this type of curry in my restaurant for special occasions as it requires a lot of labour. Oily fish like salmon, trout and mackerel work particularly well in this type of curry. Halba campur, also known as panch poran in Indian cooking, is a mix of herbs consisting of brown and black mustard seeds, plus nigella, cumin, fennel and fenugreek seeds. You can make your own mixture if you can't find it in your local Asian store, just mix together ¼ teaspoon of each spice.

----

1 Toast the ingredients for the ground spices in a dry frying pan for 1 minute until fragrant, then grind the mixture using a spice grinder until fine. Blitz the paste ingredients with a dash of water in a food processor until smooth, then transfer to a bowl and mix thoroughly with the ground spices.

2 Heat a large saucepan over a medium heat and add the oil. Sauté the curry leaves for 10 seconds until fragrant, then add the spice mixture and halba campur and cook until the oil separates. Add the tamarind and salt and cook for 1 minute.

3 Add the fish, together with 100ml of water, and cook for 2 minutes, until the fish pieces are sealed. Add the coconut milk, okra and cherry tomatoes with another 300ml of water, bring to the boil, and cook for a further 2 minutes, until the vegetables have wilted.

4 Flake through the fish with a fork to check that it is cooked, then scoop into a serving bowl, garnish with the coriander, and serve with rice.

6 tablespoons vegetable oil
2 sprigs of curry leaves, leaves
 picked (or 3 bay leaves)
1 teaspoon halba campur (see left)
2 tablespoons tamarind paste (or
 lemon or lime juice)
1½ teaspoons fine sea salt
800g salmon fillets, cut into 4cm-
 wide strips
50ml coconut milk
6 okra, diagonally sliced in half
8 cherry tomatoes
2 tablespoons finely chopped
 coriander, for garnishing

For the ground spices
2 tablespoons coriander seeds
1 teaspoon fennel seeds
½ teaspoon cumin seeds
½ teaspoon fenugreek seeds
1 teaspoon black peppercorns
5cm cinnamon
1 star anise

For the paste
3 shallots
8 dried chillies, soaked in boiling
 water for 10 minutes
4 cloves of garlic
2.5cm fresh ginger
5cm fresh turmeric (or 2 teaspoons
 ground turmeric)

Serves 4

Spicy Squid Stir-fry PAPRIK SOTONG

2 tablespoons vegetable oil
3 cloves of garlic, thinly sliced
2.5cm fresh ginger, julienned
2 stalks of lemongrass, bruised
4 kaffir lime leaves (or strips of rind
  from 2 limes)
4 bird's-eye chillies
1 red chilli, thinly and diagonally
  sliced
1 medium onion, thinly sliced
500–600g squid tubes, cleaned and
  scored
1 tablespoon oyster sauce
1 tablespoon light soy sauce
1 tablespoon fish sauce
1 teaspoon brown sugar

Serves 3–4

Squid can easily become rubbery when cooked. The best way to prevent this is to fry it on a high heat so that the squid is cooked on the outside and still soft inside. The word *paprik* derives from a Thai phrase meaning 'stir-fry', and *prik*, which means 'chilli'.

----

1 Heat a wok or a large frying pan over a high heat. Add the oil and fry the garlic, ginger and lemongrass until fragrant. Add the kaffir lime leaves, all the chillies and the onion and fry for 30 seconds, until the onion slightly wilts.

2 Now add the squid, all the sauces and the sugar, and keep frying for 1–2 minutes, until the squid pieces have curled up. Transfer to a platter and serve straight away.

Prawn & Broad Bean Stir-fry

SAMBAL UDANG DAN PETAI

3 shallots
2.5cm fresh ginger
3 cloves of garlic
6 tablespoons vegetable oil
8 tablespoons chilli paste, ready-
made from a jar or homemade (see
page 204)
1½ tablespoons brown sugar
1 teaspoon fine sea salt
2 tablespoons tamarind paste (or
lemon or lime juice)
1 teaspoon shrimp paste, dry-toasted
(or 2 tablespoons fish sauce)
600g raw king prawns, peeled
100g broad beans (or bitter beans),
blanched in boiling water for 2
minutes

Serves 3–4

Petai – sometimes known as bitter bean – is rich in protein, potassium and vitamin B6. It has a lot of health benefits, such as control of blood pressure and anaemia. I used to dislike these beans because of their strong smell, but once I became aware of the benefits, I began to eat them a lot more often. You can reduce the smell by blanching the beans in boiling water with a splash of white vinegar. You can buy *petai* in some oriental supermarkets, or you can substitute broad beans. The petai tree grows wild in Malaysian forests and has become a source of income for the Orang Asli (indigenous community) who live in the rural part of Peninsular Malaysia, on the way up to the Cameron Highlands, famous for its tea plantations. My dream would be to forage with them one day and discover unknown Malaysian herbs and spices.

----

1 Using a food processor or a hand blender, blitz together the shallots, ginger and garlic until smooth. Heat the oil in a wok or a large frying pan over a medium heat and sauté the mixture until fragrant and golden brown. Add the chilli paste, sugar, salt, tamarind and shrimp paste, then reduce the heat to low and simmer for 3 minutes, until the oil separates.

2 Add the prawns, bitter beans and 100ml of water and cook for 4 minutes, until the prawns have turned pink and are cooked. Add another 200ml of water and cook for a further minute, then turn the heat off. Transfer to a platter and serve straight away.

Scrambled Eggs with Oysters

TIRAM DAN TELUR DADAR

Every time I see oysters they remind me of a story my late mum told me when I was little. She grew up in Penang, near the beach, and one day she went out at low tide and found a lot of oysters lying around. Luckily for her, seven of them had pearls inside, which she subsequently sold (although I think she should have kept them). This simple but delicious street food dish is very popular in my home town in Penang. There's a good tip in this recipe for making oysters stay plump and juicy even after you have fried them. You can apply the same tip to any other oyster recipe.

----

1 To remove any sand or grit from the oysters, coat them with 2 tablespoons of plain flour and leave them for 2 minutes before washing them with cold water.

2 To make the oysters plump and juicy, bring 500ml of water to the boil in a saucepan and add the white vinegar. Add the oysters and blanch them for 1 minute. Use a slotted spoon to scoop them out, then place them in a small bowl of ice-cold water to prevent them continuing to cook. Set aside.

3 To make the batter, put the plain flour, cornflour and salt into a bowl with 100ml of water and mix until smooth. Add the eggs and mix them in thoroughly. Heat 1 tablespoon of oil in a 25cm frying pan. Pour in the batter mixture and sprinkle in 1 tablespoon of soy sauce. Cook the batter until crisp, then flip it over and use two wooden spoons to scramble it into smaller pieces. Turn off the heat, then scoop out the scrambled batter and put it on a plate.

4 Reheat the pan over a high heat and add the remaining tablespoon of oil. Sauté the garlic until fragrant and slightly golden brown, then add the oysters and the spring onion and cook until wilted. Splash in the remaining tablespoon of soy sauce and stir gently, then scoop out and add to the scrambled batter. Sprinkle a pinch of white pepper on top before serving.

12 oysters, shelled
2 tablespoons vegetable oil
2 tablespoons light soy sauce
3 cloves of garlic, finely chopped
1 spring onion, cut into 0.5cm slices
A pinch of white pepper

For the egg batter
4 tablespoons plain flour
4 tablespoons cornflour
½ teaspoon fine sea salt
2 eggs

To prepare the oysters
2 tablespoons plain flour
1 tablespoon white vinegar (e.g. rice vinegar)

Serves 2–3

Crispy Fried Sea Bream with Turmeric IKAN GORENG KUNYIT

3 medium whole sea bream, about 150–200g each, gutted, de-scaled and scored (or use sea bream fillets)
1 tablespoon ground turmeric
1 teaspoon fine sea salt
½ tablespoon coarsely ground black pepper
6 tablespoons vegetable oil

Serves 3–4

I was ten years old when I first attempted to fry fish with turmeric, hoping to impress my family. I was allowed into the kitchen at a young age, though most of the time I was under my mum's supervision. I coated the fish nicely with turmeric, seasoned them with salt, then fried them, and they looked so good. But to my surprise no one was willing to eat them. My mum didn't say anything, just smiled. Only then did my sister speak up – I used to argue with her a lot when I was little: 'Nobody wants to eat your fish because you haven't gutted them!' Oh, how could I have forgotten? Lesson learnt. To avoid that kind of humiliation and fuss, try this simple recipe with fish fillets and reduce the cooking time to 2 minutes on each side.

----

1 Rinse the fish with water, then rub it generously with the turmeric, salt and black pepper and leave to marinate for 10 minutes.

2 Set a large frying pan over a medium heat, add the oil, and fry the fish for 3 minutes on each side. Serve straight away.

Meat

Chicken in Soy Sauce & Honey

AYAM MASAK MADU

1 kg boneless chicken thigh pieces
2 tablespoons ground turmeric
½ teaspoon fine sea salt
6 tablespoons vegetable oil
2 shallots, finely chopped
3 cloves of garlic, finely chopped
2.5cm fresh ginger, finely chopped
2 tablespoons ground spice mix for
 meat (see page 211), mixed with
 a little water
3 tablespoons honey
150ml sweet soy sauce
½ teaspoon fine sea salt

The spices and herbs
5cm cinnamon stick
1 star anise
4 cloves
2 cardamom pods
1 pandan leaf, tied into a knot (or
 2 bay leaves)
2 sprigs of curry leaves, leaves
 picked (or 3 bay leaves)

Serves 4

This is a must-have dish when you visit a Mamak *nasi kandar* restaurant, where you can also eat rice and all sorts of other dishes with a Mamak signature twist. These famous Indian Muslim eating places are popular and unique, especially in Penang. The chicken is cooked in a reduced soy and honey sauce. At a Mamak restaurant it is usually cooked on the bone, but for this recipe I've used boneless chicken thighs, to reduce the cooking time while still giving moistness to the meat.

----

1 Put the chicken, turmeric and salt into a bowl and leave to marinate for 15 minutes.

2 Heat a large frying pan over a medium heat. Add 4 tablespoons of oil and shallow-fry the chicken for 3 minutes on each side, until golden brown. (There is no need for them to be fully cooked, as they will be cooked again in the sauce.)

3 Heat a saucepan over a medium heat. Add the remaining oil and sauté the shallots, garlic and ginger until fragrant and golden brown. Add the spices and herbs and sauté for 1 minute. Add the ground spice mix and cook for 2 minutes, then add the chicken, honey, sweet soy sauce and salt along with 200ml of water. Bring to the boil, then reduce the heat to low and simmer for 10 minutes, until the chicken pieces are thoroughly cooked. The sauce should be reduced and thickened.

4 Transfer to a serving bowl and serve with rice.

Simple Malay Chicken Curry

GULAI AYAM

There are so many different curries in Malaysia, and they are all eaten on a daily basis. This particular version lets the spices take centre stage. Like any good curry, it is a blend of spices, tamarind, and not too overpowering creamy coconut. (I prefer my curry with less coconut.) I like to serve this slightly thicker than is traditional, so that the sauce gives an extra kick to the rice accompaniment. You can also make the dish with beef, lamb, or just with vegetables, such as butternut squash, pumpkin, aubergine and sweet potato.

----

1 Blitz the onion, garlic and ginger in a food processor or with a hand blender until fine. In a bowl, mix the ground spice mix with 100ml of water.

2 Heat a saucepan over a medium heat and add the oil. Sauté the blitzed ingredients until golden brown, then add the star anise, cinnamon and pandan leaf. Fry for 30 seconds, then add the ground spice mix, tamarind and salt and cook for 2–3 minutes, until the oil separates.

3 Add the chicken pieces together with 150ml of water and simmer until the chicken is cooked through. Lastly add the coconut milk and bring to the boil. Scoop out into a bowl and serve with rice.

½ a medium onion
3 cloves of garlic
2.5cm fresh ginger
3 tablespoons ground spice mix
  for meat (see page 211)
4 tablespoons vegetable oil
1 star anise
5cm cinnamon stick
1 pandan leaf, tied in a loose knot
  (or 3 bay leaves)
2 tablespoons tamarind paste
  (or lemon or lime juice)
1 teaspoon fine sea salt
400g boneless chicken breasts,
  thinly sliced
50ml coconut milk

Serves 2–3

Spicy & Sour Beef Stew

SINGGANG DAGING

400g beef sirloin, thinly sliced
1 shallot, thinly sliced
2 cloves of garlic, thinly sliced
2.5cm fresh ginger, thinly sliced
2.5cm fresh galangal (or extra
 ginger), thinly sliced
½ teaspoon ground turmeric
2 stalks of lemongrass (use bottom
 half only), bruised
½ tablespoon coriander seeds,
 coarsely ground
4 bird's-eye chillies, bruised
2 tablespoons tamarind paste
 (or lemon or lime juice)
½ teaspoon shrimp paste,
 dry-toasted (or 2 tablespoons
 fish sauce)
1 teaspoon fine sea salt
10 cherry tomatoes

For the garnish
2 tablespoons ready-made fried
 shallots
1 spring onion, cut into 5cm strips
6 sprigs of fresh coriander
½ teaspoon chilli flakes

Serves 3–4

Singgang is very similar to Thai *tom yam* soup. It is usually cooked without turmeric, but I've added a little to give a bit of colour to the stew. It is simple to cook and ideal as a winter warmer. It can also be made with oily fish, such as salmon or mackerel, as an alternative to beef.

----

1 Put all the ingredients apart from the cherry tomatoes and the garnish into a saucepan and add 1.2 litres of water. Bring to the boil, then reduce the heat and simmer, uncovered, for 30 minutes, until the beef is tender.

2 Add the cherry tomatoes and cook for 2 minutes, until they have begun to soften. Turn off the heat and garnish with fried shallots, spring onions, coriander leaves and chilli flakes.

Chinese Chicken & Herb Stew

BAK KUT TEH AYAM

1.2kg chicken thighs, on the bone
8 cloves of garlic, crushed
1 tablespoon dark soy sauce
2 tablespoons light soy sauce
1 tablespoon oyster sauce
8 pieces of ready-made fried spongy
  tofu, cut in half
80g dried beancurd sticks, soaked
  in cold water for 1 hour and cut into
  5cm pieces
4 sprigs of fresh coriander, finely
  chopped, for garnishing
1 spring onion, cut into 0.5cm slices,
  for garnishing

Spices (or use a 70g ready-made
  bak kut teh spice pack)
1 teaspoon white peppercorns,
  lightly crushed
1 star anise
1 cinnamon stick
1 teaspoon fennel seeds
4 slices of dried liquorice root
  (gan chao)
3 slices of dried astragalus root
  (huang qi)
4 slices of dried angelica root
  (dong quai)
4 dried plum flower roots
  (dang shen)

Serves 4–6

Teh means 'tea' in Malay, and this, a herbal 'tea' simmered with meat, is a heritage dish of the Malaysian Chinese community and is well known in the Klang Valley area, about forty minutes' drive from Kuala Lumpur. It's traditionally cooked with pork, but for my version I use chicken thighs on the bone. The soup is infused with cinnamon, star anise, several types of dried roots, fennel and white pepper. Ready-made *bak kut teh* spice packs (70g) are available in Chinese supermarkets, but in case you can't find them, I've listed all the spices that you need, which need to be tied inside a piece of muslin. To get a good blend of flavours, the ingredients are simmered for two or more hours – in fact, the longer the better. I've added two different types of tofu, dried and pre-fried spongy, to give a different texture to the soup. It's usually served with rice or noodles, with a chilli dip, but I prefer it on its own in the cold winter.

----

1 Into a large pot put the chicken, garlic, soy sauces, oyster sauce and the spices, tied inside a piece of muslin. Add 2 litres of water, bring to the boil, then reduce the heat and simmer for 1 hour.

2 Add the fried spongy tofu and beancurd sticks and simmer for a further 15 minutes. Scoop out into bowls and serve, garnished with the coriander and spring onion.

Chicken Liver & Fine Green Bean Stir-fry

HATI AYAM DAN KACANG BUNCIS GORENG

I love the texture of chicken livers; they are one of my favourite ingredients. Livers are inexpensive, rich in flavour and, if cooked properly, are not rubbery in the way many British people seem to have memories of them. You can also make this dish with beef or lamb, if you prefer – both work well with the ground spices. Another good way to cook chicken livers is to coat them with turmeric and a hint of salt and deep-fry them until crisp, like my mum used to do.

----

1 Put the chicken livers, chillies, turmeric and ground spices into a bowl and leave to marinate for 5 minutes.

2 Heat a medium saucepan over a medium heat and add the marinated ingredients, coconut milk and salt, along with 200ml of water. Bring to the boil, then reduce the heat to low and simmer for 5 minutes, until the sauce is reduced to half and the livers are cooked through. Add the beans and cook for 1 minute, until they wilt slightly.

3 Transfer to a platter and serve straight away.

500g chicken livers, cut into 4cm chunks
2 green chillies, deseeded and pounded
2cm fresh turmeric, pounded (or 1 teaspoon ground turmeric)
½ tablespoon ground coriander
½ teaspoon ground cumin
½ teaspoon ground fennel
1 green cardamom pod, whole pod pounded until fine
100ml coconut milk
½ teaspoon fine sea salt
400g fine green beans, cut diagonally into 4cm pieces

Serves 2–3

Grilled Steak DAGING BAKAR

This is the dish that I think of as 'Malaysian steak'. You can either grill the beef using charcoal, or simply use a griddle pan. It is normally grilled without any seasoning, but for this recipe I season the beef with coarsely pounded coriander, ground cumin and white pepper, to add flavour. The best cut of beef to use is sirloin. Serve with a tamarind dip.

----

1 Put the coriander, cumin and peppercorns into a mortar and pound with a pestle, leaving the texture slightly coarse. Transfer to a large bowl.

2 Add the beef and salt to the bowl, and leave to marinate for 30 minutes.

3 Grill the beef for 5 minutes on each side. Then, depending on how you prefer your beef to be done, grill it for another 2 minutes or so on each side – this will give you medium rare beef (the way I like it). You can cook the beef in a heavy-duty, thick-based frying pan if you prefer. Let the pan get really hot – this will give your beef a slightly charred, sweet finish.

4 Transfer the cooked beef to a platter, cover with aluminium foil (or, to be more rustic, with a banana leaf) and let it rest for 5 minutes, then slice into 2cm-thick strips and serve with tamarind dip with diced tomato and onion (see page 210).

2 tablespoons coriander seeds
1 tablespoon cumin seeds
1 tablespoon white peppercorns
4 beef steaks, about 150g each
1½ teaspoons fine sea salt

Serves 4

Rich Lamb Curry

KERUTUP KAMBING

8 tablespoons vegetable oil
5cm cinnamon stick
2 star anise
4 green cardamom pods
1 stalk of lemongrass, bruised
2 pandan leaves, tied into a knot
 (or 4 bay leaves)
2 tablespoons tamarind paste
 (or lemon or lime juice)
1 tablespoon brown sugar
1½ teaspoons fine sea salt
1kg boneless lamb leg, cut into 4cm
 chunks
200ml coconut milk
3 tablespoons kerisik (roasted
 coconut, see page 212)

For the ground spices
5 tablespoons ground spice mix for
 aromatic beef rice and rich lamb
 curry (see page 210)

For the paste
3 shallots
10 dried chillies, soaked in boiling
 water for 10 minutes
4 cloves of garlic
5cm fresh ginger
5cm fresh galangal (or extra ginger)
5cm fresh turmeric (or 2 teaspoons
 ground turmeric)
1 medium onion
3 stalks of lemongrass
1 teaspoon shrimp paste, dry-toasted
 (or 2 tablespoons fish sauce)

- - - - - - - - - - - - - -

Serves 4–6

Kerutup (or *kerutub*) is a dish originating from Kelantan, on the beautiful east coast of Peninsular Malaysia. Similar to *rendang* (see page 96), this dish is rich in flavour and can also be made with beef, chicken, duck or even venison. This type of curry is best eaten the day after it is made.

- - - - - - - - - - - - - -

1 Blitz the paste ingredients in a food processor with a dash of water until smooth. Transfer to a bowl and mix thoroughly with the ground spice mix.

2 Heat a large saucepan over a medium heat and add the oil. Sauté the cinnamon, star anise, cardamom pods, lemongrass and pandan leaves for 2 minutes, until fragrant. The spices will infuse the oil. Add the spice paste mixture, tamarind, sugar and salt and sauté for 2–3 minutes, until the oil separates.

3 Add the lamb and stir well so that the spices coat the meat. Now add the coconut milk, along with 300ml of water, and bring to the boil, then reduce the heat to a simmer for 30 minutes, until the sauce is reduced and thickened.

4 Add the *kerisik* and stir well, then turn the heat off and transfer to a serving bowl. Serve with plain rice or steamed sticky rice (see page 144).

Nyonya Kapitan Chicken Curry

KARI AYAM KAPITAN NYONYA

Kapitan was the name given by the Portuguese colonists to the head of the Chinese community. This Peranakan heritage curry was the favourite of the *kapitan*, fusing Chinese and local Malay traditions. It is beautifully flavoured with ground spices and herbs, and the kaffir lime gives a slightly tingling sour taste to the curry. I throw in the lime leaves at the end, as I want to keep their citrusy flavour and not dilute it, which would happen if they were added at the beginning. This curry sauce is thick and full of complex flavours.

----

1 Dry-toast the spice mix in a frying pan on a medium heat for 1 minute, then transfer to a spice grinder and grind until fine.

2 Using a food processor or a hand blender, blitz together the paste ingredients with a dash of water until smooth. Transfer to a bowl and mix well with the ground spice mix.

3 Heat the oil in a saucepan over a medium heat and sauté the lemongrass for 1 minute to infuse the oil. Add the paste and spice mix and sauté for 2 minutes, until the oil separates. Add the salt, sugar and chicken and cook for 2 minutes to seal.

4 Add the coconut milk together with 300ml of water and bring to the boil, then reduce the heat to low and simmer for 10 minutes, stirring once or twice, until the chicken is cooked through.

5 Finally add the *kerisik*, lime leaves and lime juice and cook for 2 minutes, then serve with jasmine rice.

6 tablespoons vegetable oil
1 stalk of lemongrass, bruised
1½ teaspoons fine sea salt
½ tablespoon brown sugar
800g boneless chicken thighs
100ml coconut milk
3 tablespoons kerisik (roasted coconut, see page 212)
6 kaffir lime leaves, thinly sliced (or strips of rind from 2 limes)
1½ tablespoons lime juice

For the spice mix
2 tablespoons coriander seeds
½ teaspoon ground nutmeg
2 teaspoons cumin seeds
½ teaspoon fenugreek seeds
5cm cinnamon stick

For the paste
3 shallots
5 cloves of garlic
5cm fresh turmeric (or 2 teaspoons ground turmeric)
2.5cm fresh ginger
2.5cm fresh galangal (or extra ginger)
½ a medium onion
8 dried chillies, soaked in boiling water for 10 minutes
2 stalks of lemongrass
1 teaspoon shrimp paste, dry-toasted (or 2 tablespoons fish sauce)
4 crushed macadamia nuts

Serves 4–6

Perak Beef Rendang

RENDANG DAGING TOK PERAK

6 tablespoons vegetable oil
1 stalk of lemongrass, bruised
4 green cardamom pods
800g beef (rump is best)
100ml coconut milk
1 tablespoon dark coconut sugar or
  molasses sugar
1 teaspoon fine sea salt
4 tablespoons kerisik (roasted
  coconut, see page 212)
4 kaffir lime leaves, bruised (or strips
  of rind from 2 limes)

For the ground spice mix
1 tablespoon fennel seeds
2 tablespoons coriander seeds
1 teaspoon cumin seeds
1 teaspoon black peppercorns

For the spice paste
10 dried chillies, soaked in boiling
  water for 10 minutes
3 stalks of lemongrass
5cm fresh ginger
5cm fresh galangal (or extra ginger)
5cm fresh turmeric (or 2 teaspoons
  ground turmeric)
3 cloves of garlic
1 teaspoon shrimp paste, dry-toasted
  (or 2 tablespoons fish sauce)
½ a medium onion

Serves 4–6

Rendang **is a well-known Malay dish, in many ways emblematic of Malaysian cuisine. Yet since I first posted a recipe video on YouTube, debate has been raging online whether it is truly Malaysian. Well, research now suggests that it is originally from elsewhere in the Malay world – from Padang in Sumatra, now part of Indonesia. As people migrated centuries ago to what is now Malaysia, they brought their culinary heritage with them, and** *rendang* **has evolved and been popularized there. There are many different styles and traditions about making it, but this one is my favourite. Originating from the state of Perak, it combines traditional ingredients with aromatic spices, making a truly sensational dish.**

----

1 Dry-toast the spice mix ingredients in a small pan until fragrant, then grind the seeds using a spice grinder until they have turned to a fine powder. Blitz the paste ingredients in a food processor until smooth.

2 Mix the ground spice mix and the spice paste ingredients in a bowl, to form a curry paste. Heat the oil in a large saucepan and sauté the lemongrass and cardamom pods for 30 seconds to infuse the oil. Add the paste and spice mixture and sauté for about 5 minutes, until the oil separates.

3 Add the beef, coconut milk, sugar and salt along with 100ml of water, giving it all a good stir. Simmer on a low heat for 45 minutes, or until the beef is tender.

4 Finally add the *kerisik* and lime leaves and simmer for 2 minutes over a low heat. Serve with steamed jasmine rice.

Aromatic Chicken Curry

KARI AYAM

300g potatoes
6 tablespoons vegetable oil
1 star anise
5cm cinnamon stick
2 sprigs of curry leaves, leaves
  picked (or 3 bay leaves)
1 tablespoon tamarind paste
  (or lemon or lime juice)
1 teaspoon fine sea salt
800g boneless chicken thigh pieces
100ml coconut milk
4 sprigs of fresh coriander, leaves
  picked and roughly chopped

For the ground spice mix
2 tablespoons coriander seeds
2 teaspoons cumin seeds
2 teaspoons fennel seeds
1 cinnamon stick, broken into pieces
1 star anise, broken into pieces

For the spice paste
10 dried chillies, soaked in boiling
  water for 10 minutes
4 cloves of garlic
2 shallots
1.5cm fresh ginger
2.5cm fresh turmeric (or 1 teaspoon
  ground turmeric)

Serves 4–6

Many Malaysians prefer to use a ready-made curry mix because of the length of time required to prepare it from scratch. I promise that you will enjoy the end result of the herbs and spices in this recipe – an aromatic and fragrant curry. The curry paste mix can be made and then kept frozen for many weeks.

----

1 In a small saucepan of water, boil the potatoes with their skins on for 8–10 minutes, until cooked. Drain, peel and cut into small chunks, then transfer to a bowl and set aside.

2 Toast the ground spice mix ingredients in a frying pan on a medium heat for 1 minute. Transfer to the spice grinder and grind until smooth.

3 Using a food processor or a hand blender, blitz the paste ingredients with a dash of water until smooth. Transfer to a bowl and mix well with the ground spice mix.

4 Heat a saucepan over a medium heat. Add the oil and sauté the star anise and cinnamon for 30 seconds to infuse the oil. Add the paste and spice mixture and the curry leaves and sauté for 2 minutes, until the oil separates.

5 Add the tamarind and salt and cook for 1 minute, then add the chicken and cook for 2 minutes to seal. Add the coconut milk, along with 600ml of water, bring to the boil, then reduce the heat to low and simmer for 10 minutes, until the chicken is cooked.

6 Add the potatoes and cook for a further 2 minutes. Garnish with the chopped coriander and serve straight away, with jasmine or basmati rice.

Beef in Soy Sauce

DAGING MASAK KICAP

This is one of the dishes my mum used to cook at her canteen in Butterworth – she served it with tomato rice (see page 145). The dish is infused with spices and herbs and is rich in sweet soy flavour. There is a tingling chilli heat from the ground spice mix. The dish should be allowed to simmer until the beef is tender and has had time to infuse all the ingredients, by which time it simply melts in your mouth.

300g potatoes, peeled and cut into
 1cm slices
200ml vegetable oil
½ a medium onion, finely chopped
5 cloves of garlic, finely chopped
2.5cm fresh ginger, finely chopped
5cm cinnamon stick
2 star anise
4 cardamom pods
1 pandan leaf, tied in a loose knot
 (or 2 bay leaves) (optional)
2 tablespoons ground spice mix for
 meat (see page 211), mixed with
 a dash of water
½ teaspoon fine sea salt
1kg beef topside, cut into chunks
180ml sweet soy sauce
3 tablespoons coconut milk

For the garnish
6 tablespoons vegetable oil
2 sprigs of curry leaves, leaves
 picked (or 3 bay leaves)
5cm fresh ginger, julienned
1 medium red onion, cut into 0.5cm
 rings

Serves 4–6

1 Remove some of the starch from the sliced potatoes by soaking them in water for 5 minutes, then pat dry with kitchen paper.

2 Heat the oil in a frying pan over a medium heat and fry the potatoes until they are golden brown. Take them out with slotted spoon and set aside. Use the same oil to fry the garnish ingredients until crisp and golden brown. Scoop out and set aside.

3 Heat a large deep saucepan over a medium heat and add 6 tablespoons of the oil used to fry the potatoes and garnish. Add the onion, garlic and ginger and cook until fragrant. Add the cinnamon, star anise, cardamom pods and pandan leaf and cook, stirring, until the mixture turns golden.

4 Add the ground spice mix and salt and cook until the oil separates. Cook for a further 2 minutes, then add the beef and stir to coat. Add the soy sauce, coconut milk and 250ml of water, bring to the boil, then reduce the heat and simmer for 30 minutes, until the meat is tender and the sauce has thickened.

5 Remove from the heat and add the fried potatoes and the garnish ingredients, stirring well. Serve straight away.

Chicken & Shiitake Mushroom Stir-fry

AYAM GORENG CENDAWAN

8 dried shiitake mushrooms
2 tablespoons vegetable oil
1 red chilli, cut into 0.5cm slices
5 cloves of garlic, finely chopped
2.5cm fresh ginger, julienned
800g boneless chicken breasts, thinly
  sliced
4 tablespoons oyster sauce
2 tablespoons light soy sauce
1 teaspoon sesame oil
½ teaspoon white pepper
2 spring onions, cut into 0.5cm slices

Serves 4–6

Shiitake mushrooms are really meaty and have an earthy flavour, but if you can't find them, just use button or oyster mushrooms. This easy and quick stir-fry is of Malaysian Chinese heritage and can be cooked in 20 minutes. I love the smell of sautéd garlic, ginger and chilli. The trick is to infuse the oil so that when the meat is added, the flavour will stick to it, enhancing the taste.

----

1 Soak the shiitake mushrooms in boiling water for 10 minutes, until they are soft. Drain, remove the stems and cut the mushrooms in half, then transfer to a bowl and set aside.

2 Heat the oil in a wok or a large pan over a medium heat. Sauté the chilli, garlic and ginger until fragrant and golden brown. Add the chicken, oyster sauce and soy sauce, and cook for 2 minutes to seal the chicken.

3 Add the shiitake mushrooms and 100ml of water and cook for a further 3 minutes, or until the chicken is cooked. Turn off the heat and sprinkle with the sesame oil, white pepper and spring onions. Give it all a good stir and serve straight away.

Chicken in Chilli & Tomato Sauce

AYAM MASAK MERAH

This aromatic dish is infused with cinnamon and star anise, while the pandan leaf gives it a hint of nutty fragrance. If you can't find pandan leaves, use lemongrass. This dish is a favourite for a Malay wedding reception. It is usually cooked with chicken on the bone, but for this recipe I recommend boneless chicken pieces for a quicker cooking time. The dish is best served with tomato rice (see page 145).

----

1 Mix the turmeric and salt, then rub them over the chicken pieces and set aside for 5 minutes.

2 Heat the oil in a large frying pan over a medium heat and shallow-fry the chicken for 4 minutes, until brown. Fry in two or three batches – the chicken doesn't need to be fully cooked, as it will be simmered in the sauce. Take out the chicken pieces and set aside.

3 Reheat the oil in the pan and add the shallots, garlic and ginger. When the ingredients are smelling fragrant, add the pandan leaf, star anise and cinnamon and cook until the ingredients start to turn golden brown. Add the chilli paste, tomato purée, tamarind, sugar and salt and cook on a medium heat until the oil separates.

4 Add the chicken, along with 200ml of water, stir, then allow to simmer for 10 minutes, until the chicken is cooked through. Add the coconut milk and cook for 1 minute, then add the tomatoes and peas and leave to cook for 2 minutes, until wilted. Serve straight away.

½ tablespoon ground turmeric
A pinch of fine sea salt
800g boneless chicken breasts, cut into big chunks
150ml vegetable oil
2 shallots, finely chopped
4 cloves of garlic, finely chopped
2.5cm fresh ginger, finely chopped
1 pandan leaf, tied in a knot (or 1 stick of lemongrass)
2 star anise
5cm cinnamon stick
8 tablespoons chilli paste, ready-made in a jar or homemade (see page 204)
4 tablespoons tomato purée
½ tablespoon tamarind paste (or lemon or lime juice)
½ tablespoon white sugar
1 teaspoon fine sea salt
2 tablespoons coconut milk
2 tomatoes, cut into quarters
3 tablespoons frozen peas

Serves 4–6

Malaysian Portuguese Devil's Curry

KARI AYAM DEVIL

This dish originates from the Kristang Eurasian community, a settlement of mixed Portuguese and Asian descent in Malacca, who call it *cari debal* in their Creole language. The Kristang cuisine, a blend of East and West, is very underrated – it should be more widely known and celebrated, as with the traditional Nyonya cuisine. This curry is fiery hot, with a large amount of chilli, which I have reduced here, though you are welcome to add more if you wish. No coconut milk is used, only vinegar, to give a strong, sharp and pungent flavour that works well with the lemongrass, galangal and chilli.

---

1 In a bowl, soak all the mustard seeds in the vinegar for 10 minutes. Using a food processor or a hand-held blender, blitz the paste ingredients until smooth, adding a dash of water if it gets too dry.

2 Heat a small frying pan over a medium heat. Add the oil and fry the potatoes until golden brown and cooked through. Scoop out with a slotted spoon and dry with kitchen paper. Set aside.

3 Heat a large deep saucepan over a medium heat. Pour in the oil left over from frying the potatoes, then add the spice paste and sauté for 4 minutes, until it smells fragrant and the oil separates. Add the salt and sugar and cook for 1 minute, then add the chicken and cook for 3 minutes, to seal. Add the mustard seeds with their soaking vinegar, the soy sauce and 200ml of water and bring to the boil. Reduce the heat to low and simmer for 15 minutes, until the chicken is cooked.

4 Add the tomatoes, chillies and potatoes and cook for 2 minutes. Garnish with coriander and serve, with jasmine or basmati rice.

1 teaspoon black mustard seeds
1 teaspoon brown mustard seeds
100ml white vinegar
200ml vegetable oil
2 medium potatoes, peeled and cut into chunks
1 teaspoon fine sea salt
2 teaspoons brown sugar
1.2kg chicken pieces, on the bone
2 tablespoons light soy sauce
2 tomatoes, quartered
4 green or red chillies, cut on an angle into 2cm slices
4 sprigs of coriander, for garnishing

For the spice paste
15 dried chillies, soaked in boiling water for 10 minutes
3 shallots
2 stalks of lemongrass
2.5cm fresh ginger
2.5cm fresh galangal (or extra ginger)
5cm fresh turmeric (or 2 teaspoons ground turmeric)
½ a medium onion
4 cloves of garlic

Serves 4–6

Grilled Beef in Turmeric & Coconut Milk

MASAK LEMAK DAGING PANGGANG

800g beef sirloin or rump, cut into
 big chunks
3 teaspoons cumin seeds, coarsely
 pounded
1 teaspoon black peppercorns,
 coarsely ground
1½ teaspoons fine sea salt
1 tablespoon vegetable oil
500ml coconut milk
2 tablespoons tamarind paste
 (or lemon or lime juice)
1 stalk of lemongrass, bruised
500g butternut squash, diced and
 boiled for 10 minutes
6 kaffir lime leaves, thinly sliced
 (or strips of rind from 2 limes)
1 teaspoon chilli flakes, for garnishing

For the spice paste
10 red bird's-eye chillies
2 shallots
3 cloves of garlic
5cm fresh ginger
5cm fresh turmeric (or 2 teaspoons
 ground turmeric)
2 stalks of lemongrass

Serves 4–6

This recipe is a simple version of a *daging salai* (smoked beef) dish that originates from the state of Negeri Sembilan, south of Kuala Lumpur. There, on a country road out of the town of Nilai, you will find Aunty Aini's garden café, set within a homely tropical and herb garden. I make sure I visit her every time I am back in Malaysia. She serves the most wonderful *masak lemak*. The beef is smoked with dried coconut shells to give a beautiful nutty smell. The method I recommend for this recipe, however, uses unsmoked beef, which I marinate in cumin and black pepper to give a distinctive aroma and flavour that works beautifully as an alternative.

----

1 Put the beef, cumin, black pepper and salt into a bowl and mix thoroughly. Cover with clingfilm and leave to marinate in the refrigerator for 30 minutes.

2 Blitz the paste ingredients in a food processor or using a hand-held blender until smooth.

3 Set a griddle pan over a high heat until it is hot and smoking, then add the oil. Immediately put in the beef and cook for 2 minutes on each side, then turn the heat off and cover the pan with aluminium foil for 5 minutes.

4 Preheat a large deep saucepan over a medium heat. Add the coconut milk, tamarind, lemongrass, spice paste and 600ml of water. Bring to the boil, then turn the heat to low, add the beef, butternut squash and kaffir lime leaves, and simmer for 30 minutes. Garnish with chilli flakes and serve with jasmine rice.

Lamb in Cumin & Coriander Sauce

KURMA KAMBING

6 tablespoons vegetable oil
2 shallots, finely chopped
4 cloves of garlic, finely chopped
2.5cm fresh ginger, finely chopped
4 cardamom pods
4 cloves
1 star anise
5cm cinnamon stick
1 pandan leaf, tied into a knot
  (or 2 bay leaves)
5 tablespoons ground spice mix for
  meat (see page 211)
1 tablespoon tamarind paste
  (or lemon or lime juice)
1 teaspoon fine sea salt
50ml coconut milk
600g lamb, cut into small chunks
2 sprigs of mint, leaves picked

Serves 3–4

I introduced this dish at my restaurant once and it did not do well, as my customers thought it was the usual Indian korma curry, which it is not. The flavour is heavily infused with ground coriander, cumin and a hint of cardamom. You can find it in Indian canteens in Malaysia, such as those in Brickfields (Little India) in Kuala Lumpur. If you prefer, you can use beef, chicken or goat instead of lamb, and add red onions, carrots and potatoes for colour.

----

1 Heat the oil in a frying pan over a medium heat. Add the shallots, garlic, ginger, cardamom pods, cloves, star anise, cinnamon and pandan leaf and cook until fragrant. Add the ground spice mix, along with 200ml of water, the tamarind, salt and coconut milk, and cook until the oil separates.

2 Add the lamb, give it a good stir, then add 100ml of water and leave to simmer on a low heat for 30 minutes, until the meat is cooked through. Turn the heat off and sprinkle with mint leaves. Give it a final stir and serve straight away.

My Mum's Chicken Rendang

RENDANG PEDAS AYAM

Different regions of Malaysia – even different family traditions – have their own style of *rendang*. This version, however, is very precious to me, as it is my late mum's recipe. I haven't adjusted it in any way, except that I have added kaffir lime leaves instead of the traditional turmeric leaves, which I can never find in the UK. Eventually I tried growing them myself – it was successful, and now I cut the leaves and freeze them. After a long day working at her food stalls, this was my mum's quick and lazy way of making chicken rendang – putting in all the ingredients in one go. Don't be surprised by the number of chillies – she liked it very spicy! This recipe does not work well with boneless chicken breasts, as the chicken needs to be simmered for a quite a long time and it would become dry and tough. My recommendation is to do it the Malaysian way and use a whole chicken on the bone. Some people are not so keen on doing that, but trust me, the taste is a lot better. Alternatively you could use a mixture of breast and thigh joints on the bone.

----

1 Put all the spice paste ingredients into a food processor and blend until smooth.

2 Heat a wok on a high heat and add the blended ingredients, the chicken, coconut milk, sugar, salt, tamarind and lemongrass, along with 200ml of water. Bring to the boil, then turn down to a medium heat and leave to simmer for around 1 hour, remembering to stir occasionally. Cook until the oil has separated and the sauce has thickened.

3 Now add the lime leaves and the *kerisik*. Stir and cook for a further 5 minutes, then serve with rice.

1 whole chicken, about 1.5kg, cut into 12 pieces
400ml coconut milk
1 tablespoon white sugar
1 teaspoon fine sea salt
1 tablespoon tamarind paste (or lemon or lime juice)
2 stalks of lemongrass (use bottom half only), bruised
6 kaffir lime leaves, bruised (or strips of rind from 2 limes)
2 tablespoons kerisik (roasted coconut, see page 212)

For the spice paste
20 dried chillies (fewer if you prefer it not too spicy), soaked in boiling water for 10 minutes
2.5cm fresh ginger
5cm fresh galangal (or extra ginger)
2 stalks of lemongrass
4 cloves of garlic
2 shallots
½ a medium onion

Serves 6

Soy Chicken Stir-fry

AYAM GORENG KICAP

2 skinless chicken breasts, about
 200-250g each, cut into strips
1 tablespoon vegetable oil
100g mangetout

For the marinade
3 cloves of garlic, minced
2.5cm fresh ginger, minced
50ml water
200ml sweet soy sauce
2 tablespoons oyster sauce

Serves 2

I adapted this simple recipe from the chicken rice recipe that my friend, Kak Alif, taught me whilst we were at university together. She was known as the best cook amongst all the Malaysian students. Learning to cook from her was such a privilege and most of her recipes were simple, approachable and affordable which suited our student life very well. My twist is to turn her dish into a quick stir-fry.

----

1 Mix the marinade ingredients in a bowl, then add the chicken strips and leave to marinate in a fridge for 30 minutes.

2 Heat a griddle pan or frying pan over medium heat until it's hot, then add the oil.

3 Cook the marinated chicken for 3-4 minutes, lightly tossing until the chicken is cooked through and add the mangetout and any leftover marinade and cook for 2 minutes until the vegetables are slightly wilted.

4 Turn off heat and transfer to a serving platter. Serve with jasmine rice.

Grilled Chicken with Lemongrass, Turmeric & Coconut Sauce AYAM PERCIK

800g chicken breasts, butterfly cut
2 stalks of lemongrass (use bottom
  half only), puréed
1 teaspoon ground turmeric
1 teaspoon fine sea salt

For the sauce
4 shallots, peeled
3 cloves of garlic
2.5cm fresh ginger
2 stalks of lemongrass (use bottom
  half only)
3 tablespoons vegetable oil
4 tablespoons chilli paste, ready-
  made from a jar or homemade
  (see page 204)
¼ teaspoon ground turmeric
1 tablespoon tamarind paste
  (or lemon or lime juice)
½ teaspoon fine sea salt
200ml coconut milk

This dish is ideal for a barbecue, served with a crunchy salad or, like I do in my restaurant, with blanched spinach. The strong and zesty flavour of lemongrass makes the chicken really tasty. I recommend marinating it for at least an hour, but if you have time and plan ahead, you can marinate it overnight to allow the meat to absorb all the flavours. I make the sauce slightly less spicy compared to the usual level of heat used in Malaysia. You can roughly chop some fresh bird's-eye chillies and sprinkle them on top of the dish if you want it more fiery.

Serves 4

1 Put the chicken into a bowl with the puréed lemongrass, turmeric and salt and leave to marinate for 1 hour.

2 Get the barbecue or griddle pan ready and cook the chicken for 4 minutes on each side, until nicely charred and cooked through. Transfer to a platter and cover with aluminium foil to keep it warm.

3 To make the sauce, blitz the shallots, garlic, ginger and lemongrass in a blender until fine. Heat a medium saucepan over a medium heat, then add the oil and sauté the puréed ingredients until fragrant. Add the chilli paste, turmeric, tamarind and salt, and cook for 2 minutes. Now add the coconut milk and bring to the boil.

4 Pour the sauce over the grilled chicken, and serve straight away.

Fried Spiced Chicken

AYAM GORENG BEREMPAH

800g boneless chicken thighs
4 tablespoons vegetable oil

For the marinade
30g fresh ginger
20g fresh galangal (or extra ginger)
3 cloves of garlic
2 banana shallots
4 tablespoons ground spice mix
 for meat (see page 211)
4 sprigs of curry leaves
2 teaspoons sea salt
2 tablespoons coconut milk
½ tablespoon lime juice
1 teaspoon brown sugar

Serves 4–6

In Malaysia this easy, classic fried chicken recipe is normally cooked with chicken on the bone, but it is a lot quicker to fry it you use boneless chicken thighs. Chicken breast is not the best option, as it can easily overcook and turn out dry. This recipe is great for a summer barbecue, and if you are not keen on shallow-frying, cook them in the oven at a temperature of 200°C/fan 180°C/gas mark 6 for 20 minutes, or until the chicken is cooked. Drizzle with a bit of oil before baking.

----

1 Purée the ginger, galangal, garlic and shallots and combine with all the remaining marinade ingredients in a bowl. Add the chicken pieces, stir to coat, then cover and set aside for a minimum of 1 hour, or overnight, in the fridge.

2 Heat the oil in a large frying pan or a wok over a low heat and fry the chicken for about 6 minutes on each side. Serve at once.

Beef & Ginger Stir-fry

DAGING GORENG HALIA

800g beef topside, cut into 2cm slices
2 tablespoons vegetable oil
1 red chilli, thinly sliced
3 cloves of garlic, finely chopped
5cm fresh ginger, peeled and thinly
 sliced
½ teaspoon ground turmeric
1 medium onion, thinly sliced
2 spring onions, cut into 1cm slices

For the marinade
4 tablespoons oyster sauce
1 teaspoon sesame oil
3 tablespoons light soy sauce
½ tablespoon coarsely ground black
 pepper
5cm fresh ginger, very finely
 chopped

Serves 4

Ginger is a staple herb in all Malaysian cuisine, whatever the style. I once ran an event with James Wong at the Edinburgh Botanic Garden, which focused just on the ginger family of plants. Apparently there are over 1,300 related species, and yet we use so few of them in cooking. In Malaysia we also use a variety of ginger flower, sometimes known as torch ginger, but here I am using the common ginger root that you can find in your local supermarket. The trick with peeling it is to scrape it with a teaspoon – much easier and less wasteful than using a knife. Here the ginger brings a fresh and vibrant edge to the wok-fried beef, making it a very simple and quick dish to cook after a long day at work.

----

1 Mix the marinade ingredients in a bowl, then add the beef pieces and leave to marinate at room temperature for 30 minutes.

2 Heat a wok or a large deep frying pan until it's hot and add the oil. Sauté the chilli, garlic and ginger until fragrant and golden brown. Add the marinated beef and the turmeric and stir continuously for 5 minutes, until the beef is sealed.

3 Add the onion and spring onions and stir-fry for a further minute. Turn on to a platter and serve straight away.

Vegetables

Mango Salad KERABU MANGGA

This recipe is more of a fusion than a traditional recipe, and uses ingredients that you can easily pick up at your local supermarket. In Malaysia, a traditional salad is very simple, comprising sprigs of cassava leaves and cashew leaves or raw bamboo shoots, accompanied by a sambal. Nothing can beat that, although this comes close.

----

1 Put the mangoes, tomatoes, shallot, lime juice, sea salt, dried shrimps and fish sauce (if using) into a bowl and gently but thoroughly mix with your fingers or two wooden spoons.

2 Transfer to a serving platter or bowl and sprinkle with the black pepper, chillies, crushed peanuts and coriander. Serve straight away.

700–800g unripened (firm and green, not soft and juicy) mangoes, peeled and julienned
2 tomatoes, deseeded and thinly sliced
½ a shallot, thinly sliced
2 tablespoons lime juice
½ teaspoon fine sea salt
1 teaspoon coarsely ground black pepper
2 red chillies, deseeded and pounded until fine
4 tablespoons crushed peanuts
8 sprigs of fresh coriander, leaves picked

Optional ingredients
4 tablespoons dried shrimps, soaked in warm water for 10 minutes
1 tablespoon fish sauce

Serves 4

Green Bean Salad

KERABU KACANG PANJANG

400g fine green beans, cut into 4cm
  lengths
10 cherry tomatoes, halved
50g roasted peanuts, crushed
2 sprigs of Thai basil, leaves picked
  (or regular basil)

For the dressing
1 red chilli, deseeded and coarsely
  pounded
3 cloves of garlic, coarsely pounded
2 tablespoons dried shrimps, soaked
  in warm water for 10 minutes
  (optional)
1 tablespoon palm sugar or brown
  sugar
1 tablespoon lime juice
1 tablespoon fish sauce

Serves 2–3

This is a quick salad that makes a good side dish. I blanch the beans to preserve the nutrients and bring out their strong green colour. You can make the dish vegetarian by replacing the dried shrimps with roughly chopped pre-fried spongy tofu and the fish sauce with salty soy sauce. To save time, you can use pre-roasted, salted peanuts.

----

1 In a medium saucepan, bring 500ml of water to the boil and blanch the beans for 15 seconds, until slightly wilted. Immediately transfer them to ice-cold water and let them soak for a minute. Drain and put into a bowl.

2 Add the tomatoes and all the dressing ingredients to the beans and mix gently but thoroughly. Transfer to a serving platter and sprinkle over the peanuts and basil leaves. Serve straight away.

Watercress Salad

KERABU PEGAGA

I was in Paris's Indian Quarter, shopping for my European cooking tour, when I found pennywort for sale, and it gave me the idea of including this recipe in the book. Pennywort is available in many Asian shops, but it can be replaced with watercress if you can't find any. It tastes slightly more bitter than watercress, which is peppery; however, the texture is similar. You can add 2 tablespoons of dried shrimps or fried anchovies to the salad, if you want to add another Malaysian flavour and texture to the dish.

----

1 Remove the roots from the pennywort but keep the stems. To clean the pennywort, soak it in a bowl of cold water for 5 minutes. Remove from the water and shake it a little, then hold it under cold running water for 30 seconds to remove any remaining soil.

2 Pound the onion, ginger and chilli in a pestle and mortar until fine, then put into a bowl. Add the pennywort, *kerisik*, lime juice, salt and sugar and mix thoroughly. Serve straight away.

2 bunches of watercress or pennywort, about 300g
½ a medium onion
2.5cm fresh ginger
1 red chilli, deseeded
2 tablespoons kerisik (roasted coconut, see page 212)
½ tablespoon lime juice
Fine sea salt, to taste
½ teaspoon white sugar

Serves 2–3

Nyonya Vermicelli Noodle Salad

KERABU BIHUN NYONYA

This is an aromatic noodle salad that is served cold. *Belacan*, or shrimp paste, is one of the key ingredients in most of the Nyonya dishes, equivalent to fish sauce in Thai cuisine. The combination of the noodles and the beansprouts gives contrasting texture to the salad.

---

1 Blitz the paste ingredients in a food processor or with a hand blender until smooth. Heat a small frying pan over a medium heat, then add the oil and sauté the paste for 2 minutes, until fragrant. Scoop out into a small bowl and leave to cool down completely.

2 Bring 1.5 litres of water to the boil in a medium saucepan, turn the heat off and blanch the noodles for 2 minutes, until soft. Drain, then rinse under cold water and set aside.

3 Put the saucepan back on a medium heat and add 500ml of water. Bring to the boil, then blanch the prawns until they have turned pink and are cooked. Scoop out with a slotted spoon and drop them into a bowl of ice-cold water for 1 minute. Remove and set aside.

4 Put the noodles, prawns, tofu, beansprouts, ginger flower purée, sugar, salt and lime juice into a serving bowl and stir to coat all the ingredients well. Add the shallots, coriander and kaffir lime leaves, then gently toss the salad one last time and serve straight away.

2 tablespoons vegetable oil
150g rice vermicelli noodles
200g raw king prawns, peeled
6 pieces of ready-made fried spongy tofu, each cut into 4
100g beansprouts, blanched in boiling water for 10 seconds
1 tablespoon ginger flower purée (or 2.5cm fresh galangal or ginger, peeled and puréed)
1 tablespoon brown sugar
1 teaspoon fine sea salt
2 tablespoons lime juice
3 tablespoons ready-made fried shallots
10 sprigs of fresh coriander, leaves picked and roughly chopped
6 kaffir lime leaves, thinly sliced (or strips of rind from 2 limes)

For the paste
2 shallots
3 cloves of garlic
2.5cm fresh ginger
2 stalks of lemongrass (use bottom half only)
2 red chillies, deseeded
1 teaspoon shrimp paste, dry-toasted (or 2 tablespoons fish sauce)
10g dried shrimps, soaked in warm water for 10 minutes (optional)

Serves 3–4

Malay Vegetable Dhal Curry

GULAI DALCA

300g lentils, soaked in water for a minimum of 4 hours or overnight

1 pandan leaf, tied in a knot (or 2 bay leaves)

1½ tablespoons ready-made ground spice mix for meat (see page 211)

½ teaspoon ground turmeric

150ml coconut milk

2 tablespoons tamarind paste (or lemon or lime juice)

5cm cinnamon stick

2 star anise

1 teaspoon fine sea salt

1 medium potato, peeled and cut into small chunks

1 carrot, cut into 4cm long thin wedges

150g aubergines, cut into small chunks

1 small green mango, cut into small chunks

2 green chillies, deseeded and split lengthwise

100g fine green beans, cut into 2.5cm pieces

For the garnish

3 tablespoons vegetable oil

½ a medium red onion, cut into rings

3 dried chillies

2 sprigs of curry leaves (or 3 bay leaves)

Serves 2–3

This is my late mum's recipe. She used to cook the vegetables with beef on the bone to add more flavour to the curry, but for my version I just use vegetables, so it works for vegetarians and vegans. The dhal lentils have to be soaked for at least 4 hours before they can be cooked. Green mangoes are smaller in size than the regular ones, and are available in Asian groceries. They are unripe and sour, adding a distinctive flavour to the curry. If you can't find green mangoes, use a firm green avocado instead.

----

1 Bring 1 litre of water to the boil in a medium pan. Add the drained lentils and the pandan knot and boil for 15 minutes, until the lentils are soft and slightly mushy. Add the ground spice mix, turmeric, coconut milk, tamarind, cinnamon, star anise and salt. Cook for 5 minutes over a medium heat, then add the potato, carrot, aubergine, mango, chillies and beans.

2 Cook for 5–10 minutes, until the potato and aubergine are soft. If the sauce starts to get dry, add more water. Adjust the seasoning with salt as necessary, then turn off the heat and transfer the curry to a bowl.

3 Heat the oil for the garnish in a medium frying pan. Add all the garnish ingredients at once and fry for 2 minutes, until the onion is golden brown. Take out the ingredients with a slotted spoon and sprinkle over the curry. Serve straight away.

Pumpkin in Turmeric & Coconut Milk

MASAK LEMAK LABU

500g pumpkin, peeled and cut into
  4cm chunks
3 cloves of garlic, pounded to a
  paste
2.5cm fresh turmeric, pounded
  to a paste (or 1 teaspoon ground
  turmeric)
1 medium red onion, cut into 8
  wedges
1 teaspoon fine sea salt
300ml coconut milk
4 kaffir lime leaves, thinly sliced (or
  strips of rind from 2 limes)

Serves 2–3

Except among certain Hindu and Buddhist communities in Malaysia who are vegetarian, vegetables are normally served as side dishes, though this simple recipe is also suitable for vegetarians – and vegans – as a main dish. You can either boil the pumpkin or lightly grill it, to give a charred effect. Fresh turmeric leaves are normally added to this dish to add another flavour, but as an alternative here I've used kaffir lime leaves, which are easier to obtain.

----

1 In a medium saucepan, boil the pumpkin in 500ml of water for 8–10 minutes until cooked, then drain.

2 Put the pumpkin into a medium saucepan with 500ml of water and all the rest of the ingredients except for the lime leaves. Bring to the boil over a medium heat, then reduce the heat and simmer for 5 minutes, stirring once or twice.

3 Add the lime leaves and cook for a further minute, then serve.

Green Bean & Turmeric Stir-fry

KACANG GORENG KUNYIT

This is a quick vegetarian stir-fry that can be cooked in minutes, and you can add fresh prawns, crispy fried anchovies or dried shrimps if you like. You can use carrots, mangetout or asparagus as alternatives to beans.

----

1 Soak the beans in 500ml of cold water with a pinch of salt for 3 minutes to remove any dirt, then drain and set aside.

2 Heat a wok or a large frying pan over a high heat. Add the oil and sauté the garlic and chilli until golden brown. Add the beans, salt and turmeric and fry for 2 minutes, until the beans are slightly wilted.

3 Push the beans to one side and crack in the egg, stirring. Let it scramble, then mix with the beans. Cook for 1 minute, then transfer to a serving platter and serve straight away.

500g fine green beans, cut
 diagonally into 4cm pieces
A pinch of fine sea salt
1 tablespoon vegetable oil
2 cloves of garlic, finely chopped
½ a red chilli, thinly sliced
½ teaspoon fine sea salt
½ teaspoon ground turmeric
1 egg

Serves 2–3

Aubergine Stir-fry

SAMBAL TERUNG

Cooking aubergines can be a bit tricky, as they can turn mushy if they are overcooked. In this recipe, I precook the aubergines to avoid this. This dish is made with dried shrimps, which are there to give extra flavour, but you can do without them if you wish.

----

1 Heat 1 tablespoon of oil in a wok or a large frying pan over a medium heat. Add the aubergines and salt and cook for 3–4 minutes, until wilted.

2 Pound the garlic and ginger together until fine, using a pestle and mortar. Reheat the wok or frying pan over a high heat and add the remaining 2 tablespoons of oil. When it is hot and slightly smoking, add the pounded garlic and ginger and the shallots, and stir-fry until fragrant and golden brown. Add the dried shrimps (if using) and continue stirring for a further 30 seconds.

3 Add the chilli paste, tamarind, sugar and 100ml of water, bring to the boil, then reduce the heat and simmer until the sauce is reduced to half. Add the fried aubergines and continue stirring for 1 minute more.

4 Scoop the aubergines on to a platter and serve straight away.

3 tablespoons vegetable oil
600g aubergines, cut into small chunks
½ teaspoon fine sea salt
3 cloves of garlic
2.5cm fresh ginger
2 shallots, thinly sliced
15g dried shrimps, soaked in warm water for 5 minutes and drained (optional)
6 tablespoons chilli paste, ready-made from a jar or homemade (see page 204)
½ tablespoon tamarind paste (or lemon or lime juice)
1 tablespoon brown sugar

Serves 4

Quick Cauliflower & Broccoli Stir-fry

SAYUR GORENG

1 teaspoon ground turmeric
3 tablespoons light soy sauce
1 tablespoon vegetable oil
2 cloves of garlic, finely chopped
150g cauliflower, cut into small
  chunks
150g broccoli, cut into small chunks
100g carrots, cut in half lengthways
  and diagonally sliced 0.5cm thick
½ teaspoon chilli flakes

Serves 2–3

This is a very quick stir-fry that uses turmeric, soy sauce and chilli flakes for flavouring, but if you don't like chilli flakes, you can add coarsely ground black pepper to give a bit of spicy heat to the vegetables. When frying vegetables like broccoli and cauliflower, turn the heat up high – it will cook the vegetables beautifully, keeping them crunchy inside.

----

1 Put the turmeric and soy sauce into a small bowl and mix with 50ml of water.

2 Heat a wok or a large frying pan over a high heat. Add the oil and sauté the garlic until golden brown, then add the cauliflower, broccoli and carrots. Cook for 1 minute, then add the turmeric and soy mixture.

3 Fry for 2 minutes, stirring once or twice, then scoop on to a serving platter and sprinkle chilli flakes on top. Serve straight away.

Steamed Pak Choy SAYUR STIM BERSOS TIRAM

A Malaysian Chinese friend showed me this easy way to cook pak choy. Instead of stir-frying, which can make the green part overcook easily, steaming is the best way to keep the nutrients and colour. I add chilli slices to give a bit of heat to the dish, and also to bring out the green colour and look rather attractive on the plate, but you can leave them out if you prefer it without too much spice.

----

1 Cut the pak choy into single stems and wash thoroughly.

2 Place the leaves on a plate or tray that will fit your steamer. Sprinkle the garlic and chilli on top and steam for 5 minutes, until the pak choy has wilted.

3 Take out of the steamer and sprinkle with the mushroom or oyster sauce and sesame oil. Serve straight away.

300g pak choy
2 cloves of garlic, finely chopped
1 red chilli, thinly sliced
2 tablespoons mushroom or oyster sauce
1 teaspoon sesame oil

Serves 2

1 Steamed Pak Choy
2 Quick Cauliflower & Broccoli Stir-fry
3 Stir-fried Okra

Stir-Fried Okra KACANG BENDI GORENG

2 tablespoons vegetable oil, plus
½ teaspoon for scrambling the egg
1 red chilli, diagonally cut into 0.5cm
slices
1 shallot, thinly sliced into 0.5cm rings
2 cloves of garlic, thinly sliced
300g okra, cut both ends and
diagonally sliced in half
1 tablespoon tamarind paste
(or lemon or lime juice)
2 tablespoons light soy sauce
1 egg

Serves 2

I make this as a vegetarian stir-fry, but in Malaysia fried crispy anchovies are added for flavouring and texture. I add tamarind to prevent the okra becoming slimy, and lime or lemon juice can also prevent it. You can make it without the egg if you like.

----

1 Heat a wok or a large frying pan. Add the 2 tablespoons of oil and sauté the chilli for 10 seconds, to infuse the oil.

2 Add the shallot and garlic and sauté until golden brown, then add the okra, tamarind and soy sauce and fry for 2 minutes, until the okra has begun to wilt.

3 Using a fish slice or wooden spoon, push everything to one side of the wok or frying pan and drizzle the ½ teaspoon oil into the cleared area. Crack in the egg and let it scramble, then mix the egg and okra together and fry for a further 30 seconds.

4 Scoop out on to a platter and serve.

Spinach Stir-fry BAYAM GORENG

This simple stir-fry is ideal as a side dish for curries. Instead of spinach, you can use pak choy, or any other type of greens from an oriental supermarket. To make the dish evenly spicy, it is best to fry the chilli first, before adding the garlic, so that the oil will be infused with the heat from the chilli – though with the amount of chilli I suggest, it will not be overpowering. It is more about subtlety, and is just right to balance out the garlic and soy sauce flavours.

400g spinach
1 tablespoon vegetable oil
½ a red chilli, thinly sliced
3 cloves of garlic, finely chopped
½ a medium onion, thinly sliced
2 tablespoons light soy sauce

Serves 4

1 Trim the bottom of the spinach stalks and wash the leaves well. There is no need to dry them, as the water remaining on them will help to create the sauce.

2 Heat the oil in a wok or a large frying pan over a high heat. Sauté the chilli for abut 10 seconds, then add the garlic and onion and cook until golden brown. Add the spinach and soy sauce and cover with a lid for 2 minutes, to help the spinach to wilt evenly, then take off the lid and give it all a good stir.

3 Transfer to a bowl and serve.

Eggs in Chilli Sambal

SAMBAL TUMIS TELUR

6 tablespoons vegetable oil
4 shallots, 2 cut into 0.5m rings and the others left whole
3 cloves of garlic
2.5cm fresh ginger
6 tablespoons chilli paste, ready-made from a jar or homemade (see page 204)
2 tablespoons tamarind paste (or lemon or lime juice)
1 tablespoon brown sugar
½ teaspoon fine sea salt
½ teaspoon shrimp paste, dry-toasted (or 2 tablespoons fish sauce)
4 eggs
1 large onion, sliced into thin rings
4 sprigs of fresh coriander, leaves picked
½ teaspoon chilli flakes

Serves 2–3

This is my all-time favourite of all the dishes cooked by my late mum. Every time I flew back to Penang for a holiday she would ask me which dish I wanted her to make, and I would always pick this one. Once she remarked, 'You came all the way from the UK and all you want is this?' To which I replied, 'Well, no one cooks it like you do!' She was chuffed, and cooked a few other dishes to go with it to welcome me home including beef in soy sauce. This is no ordinary *sambal tumis telur*. Most Malaysians would boil or fry the eggs before adding them to the sauce. However, the beauty of this recipe is that the eggs are cooked in the chilli sambal itself, to give them extra flavour.

----

1 Heat the oil in a frying pan over a medium heat and fry the shallot rings until golden brown. Scoop out with slotted spoon and dab with kitchen paper. Set aside.

2 Using a hand blender, purée the garlic, ginger and the remaining shallots with a dash of water until smooth. Heat the leftover oil in a frying pan over a medium heat and sauté the puréed ingredients until fragrant and golden brown. Add the chilli paste and simmer over a low heat until the oil separates, then add the tamarind, sugar, salt and shrimp paste and cook until the oil separates again. Add 300ml of water, bring to the boil, then reduce the heat to low.

3 Crack the eggs into the sauce and cook for 3–4 minutes. The dish is ready when the eggs are cooked in the sauce and the whites are firm. If you prefer your egg yolks fully cooked, leave it to simmer on a low heat for further 3–4 minutes.

4 Garnish with the fried shallots, coriander and chilli flakes, and serve.

Malaysian Omelette TELUR DADAR

4 eggs
1 medium red onion, diced
1 red chilli, cut into 0.5cm slices
½ teaspoon coarsely ground black
  pepper
¼ teaspoon fine sea salt
2 tablespoons vegetable oil

Serves 2

This omelette is a favourite dish for Malaysians. It's not included on the menu at my restaurant, but whenever my fellow Malaysians visit, there is always a special request for it. This simple dish is served as an accompaniment to other main dishes. Two ingredients that are essential are the onion and chilli, but you can use additional ingredients if you like, such as chopped spring onions and sliced mushrooms. I like my omelette moderately spicy, but if you prefer yours very spicy, add some chopped bird's-eye chillies.

----

1 Crack the eggs into a bowl and whisk gently with a fork. Add the onion, chilli, black pepper and salt and mix thoroughly.

2 Heat the oil in a 25cm frying pan over a medium heat. When it is hot enough, pour the eggs gently into the pan and reduce the heat to low. Use a fork to spread out the chilli slices evenly. You can use a different size of frying pan, but the cooking time may be different – it will take longer using a smaller pan, and less time using a bigger one.

3 Cover the frying pan with a lid or plate and cook for 2 minutes. Covering the pan makes the omelette cook more quickly and firms up the top. Flip over and cook for a further 2 minutes.

4 Transfer to a plate, cut into 8 pieces, like a pizza, and serve.

Poached Duck Eggs in Turmeric Sauce

MASAK LEMAK TELUR ITIK

Duck eggs are rich in flavour and high in protein. My late parents kept ducks when I was little, and it was my duty to collect the eggs every morning. It wasn't my favourite morning chore, especially when I was chased by the ducks! The eggs were sold to the villagers and my mum pickled any leftovers. If you can't find duck eggs, use hen's eggs instead. As for the number of chillies, add fewer if you prefer things less spicy.

----

1 Using a food processor or hand blender, blitz the paste ingredients with a dash of water until smooth.

2 Heat a medium saucepan over a medium heat and add the paste, together with the coconut milk, bruised lemongrass, tamarind and salt. Pour in the 400ml of boiling water, give a good stir and bring to the boil, then reduce the heat to low.

3 Crack one of the eggs into a cup and gently pour it into the sauce. Repeat with the rest of the eggs. They should take around 2 minutes to cook. Ensure that the sauce doesn't boil away, as this can make the eggs look a bit scruffy round the edge. Once cooked, scoop out the eggs with a slotted spoon and place in a serving bowl.

4 Add the cherry tomatoes and lime leaves to the sauce and cook for a minute over a medium heat. Gently pour the sauce over the eggs, and serve straight away.

300ml coconut milk
1 stalk of lemongrass (use bottom half only), bruised
1½ tablespoons tamarind paste (or lemon or lime juice)
½ teaspoon fine sea salt
4 large duck eggs
400ml boiling water
8 cherry tomatoes
4 kaffir lime leaves, thinly sliced (or strips of rind from 2 limes)

For the spice paste
10 green bird's-eye chillies
2 shallots
3 cloves of garlic
5cm fresh turmeric (or 2 teaspoons ground turmeric)
2 stalks of lemongrass (use bottom half only)

Serves 2–3

Rice & Noodles

Perfect White Rice NASI PUTIH

500g rice
2 pandan leaves, tied in knots (or
 3 bay leaves) (optional)

Serves 4–6

Rice is a staple food for Malaysians, and the basic rule in a Malaysian kitchen is that you must know how to cook rice properly. Nowadays, people use a rice cooker, which is easier, and the rice can be kept warm all day. The cooked rice should be fluffy, and then slightly sticky for jasmine rice and dry for basmati and long-grain. The rice will be better if you soak it in water for 20 minutes before cooking. Malaysians wash it at least three times, until the water runs clear. The rice should be cooked with just enough water for it to absorb the liquid thoroughly and for the middle part of the rice grain to be well cooked. Once cooked, leave it to rest for 15 minutes, covered, so that the rice can absorb moisture from the steam trapped inside the pan. You can infuse the rice with herbs and spices, such as pandan or bay leaves, cinnamon, star anise, cardamom and many more.

----

1 Put the rice into a bowl, cover it with cold water and let it soak for 20 minutes.

2 Drain, then put the rice and pandan knots into a deep saucepan with 1.2 litres of water. Place on a medium heat and bring to the boil, then reduce the heat and cook for 8 minutes, stirring once or twice.

3 Turn off the heat, cover with clingfilm or aluminium foil to trap the steam, and set aside for 15 minutes. Remove the pandan knots and serve straight away.

Tomato Rice

NASI TOMATO

This rice is often cooked at Malay wedding receptions, and my mum served it with chicken in chilli and tomato sauce (see page 103), beef in soy sauce (see page 100) and dhal curry (see page 126) at her canteen at the local council office in Butterworth, which served more than 1,000 people. She was in charge of the kitchen, and my dad handled the front of house. It was at the beginning of the 1990s and they were famous in the area for serving good food. My mum was fussy about the food that was served there, and if she didn't like it, she told the chefs right to their faces. Not because she was arrogant but because she wanted them to cook it right, have a passion for it and be proud of their food. This is her recipe, and I helped her cook this many times.

----

1 Heat a large deep saucepan over a medium heat. Add the ghee and sauté the raisins and almond flakes for 20 seconds, then scoop out with a slotted spoon and put them into a bowl.

2 Add the onion to the ghee remaining in the pan and sauté until golden brown, then add the garlic, ginger, cinnamon, cardamoms, cloves, star anise and pandan knots and sauté for 1 minute, until fragrant.

3 Now add the tomato purée, tomato soup and evaporated milk. Bring to the boil and add the rice, salt and rose water. Mix thoroughly, then add 900ml of water. Bring to the boil again, then turn down the heat to low. Cover with a lid and cook for 8 minutes, stirring once or twice. Turn the heat off, cover the saucepan with aluminium foil and leave for 15 minutes.

4 Sprinkle over the mint leaves, raisins and almond flakes and give a good stir, then transfer to a platter and serve straight away.

250g ghee (or butter)
50g raisins
25g almond flakes
1 medium onion, diced
4 cloves of garlic, finely chopped
2.5cm fresh ginger, finely chopped
5cm cinnamon stick
4 cardamom pods
4 cloves
1 star anise
2 pandan leaves, tied into a knot (or 2 bay leaves)
1 tablespoon tomato purée
400ml tinned tomato soup
100ml evaporated milk
500g basmati rice, washed and soaked in cold water for 20 minutes
1½ teaspoons fine sea salt
1 tablespoon rose water
4 sprigs of mint, leaves picked

Serves 4–6

Famous Penang Wok-fried Flat Noodles with Prawns CHAR KUEY TEOW

200g dried flat rice noodles, 8 or 10mm wide
2 tablespoons vegetable oil, plus extra for scrambling the egg
3 cloves of garlic, finely chopped
10 raw king prawns, peeled
10 fresh cockles, shells removed (traditional, but optional)
2 tablespoons chilli paste, ready-made from a jar or homemade (see page 204)
3 tablespoons light soy sauce
3 tablespoons sweet soy sauce
1 egg
125g beansprouts
50g kow choi (garlic or Chinese chives) or spring onions
½ teaspoon sesame oil
A pinch of ground white pepper

Serves 2

This is a Malaysian street food delight, originally from my home town of Penang and well known for its smoky and charred flavour. This is one of the top five dishes that I introduce to westerners as the ultimate Malaysian food. To give the noodles a really smokey flavour, you need to get the flame into the wok, but this is very difficult without proper training and practice. Dried flat rice noodles come in different widths, but the 10mm-wide size is the best and most authentic one to use. The noodles have to be fried on a high heat. If you can't find garlic chives, use spring onions instead.

----

1 Bring plenty of water to the boil in a medium saucepan and turn off the heat. Blanch the noodles for 8 minutes without the lid, drain and run cold water over them, then drain again and set aside.

2 Heat a wok or a large frying pan over a high heat and add the 2 tablespoons of oil. Sauté the garlic for 5 seconds or so, then add the prawns and cockles. Cook until the prawns turn pink. Add the chilli paste and fry for 30 seconds, then add the noodles and the two soy sauces. Fry for 2 minutes, until the noodles have soaked up the sauce.

3 Push the noodles to one side of the wok and drizzle in a little more oil. Break in the egg and let it scramble, then stir into the noodles. Add the beansprouts and chives and cook for 1 minute, then turn off the heat, drizzle with the sesame oil, give it all a good stir and transfer to a platter or shallow bowl.

4 Sprinkle with the pepper and serve straight away.

Prawn Curry Laksa

KARI LAKSA UDANG

I have taught this dish many times at my cookery classes and it has never failed to impress my students and become an instant hit. The blend of spices and the heat from the dried chillies, together with the coconut milk, makes the dish creamy and aromatically spicy.

----

1 Purée all the paste ingredients in a food processor until smooth.

2 Put the vermicelli noodles into a bowl and add 1 litre of boiling water. Blanch for 2 minutes, then drain. Transfer the noodles into a bowl of ice-cold water for 3 minutes, then drain again and set aside.

3 In a frying pan, dry-toast the spice mix ingredients on a medium heat for 30 seconds, then transfer to a spice grinder and grind until fine.

4 In a bowl, mix together thoroughly the blended spice paste, ground spice mix and ground turmeric.

5 Heat a saucepan over a medium heat. Add the oil and sauté the spice paste mix for 2 minutes, until fragrant. Add the prawns and cook for 2 minutes, until they have turned pink and are cooked. Add the salt, sugar and coconut milk, along with 750ml of water, and bring to the boil.

6 Reduce the heat to low and add the spinach, tofu, beansprouts, drained noodles and lime juice. Cook for 2 minutes, then transfer to a bowl and serve.

150g vermicelli noodles
½ teaspoon ground turmeric
6 tablespoons vegetable oil
12 raw king prawns, peeled
1½ teaspoons fine sea salt
1 teaspoon white sugar
100ml coconut milk
100g spinach, cut into 10cm strips
6 pieces of ready-made fried spongy tofu, each cut into 4
100g beansprouts
Juice of 1 lime

For the spice paste
8 dried chillies, soaked in boiling water for 10 minutes
3 shallots
4 cloves of garlic
2.5cm fresh ginger
2 stalks lemongrass (use bottom half only)
½ teaspoon shrimp paste, dry-toasted (or fish sauce)

For the ground spice mix
1 tablespoon coriander seeds
1 teaspoon cumin seeds
1 star anise
1 cinnamon stick
½ teaspoon black peppercorns
2 green cardamom pods

Serves 2–3

Penang Noodle Soup with Aromatic Fish Stock ASSAM LAKSA

600g mackerel fillets
4 sprigs of Vietnamese coriander
  (or basil), leaves picked off the stem
4 teaspoons ginger flower purée
  (or lemongrass purée)
4 tablespoons tamarind paste
  (or lemon or lime juice)
1½ teaspoons fine sea salt
1 teaspoon white sugar
600g thick 'ready to eat' udon rice
  noodles

For the spice paste
3 shallots
2 stalks of lemongrass (use bottom
  half only)
2.5cm fresh galangal (or ginger)
8 dried chillies, soaked in boiling
  water for 10 minutes
1 teaspoon shrimp paste, dry-toasted
  (or 2 tablespoons fish sauce)

For the garnish
100g pineapple, sliced into thin
  wedges
½ cucumber, julienned
1 medium red onion, sliced into thin
  rings
2 red chillies, deseeded and thinly
  sliced
4 sprigs of mint, leaves picked and
  roughly chopped
2 sprigs of Vietnamese coriander
  (or basil), leaves picked and roughly
  chopped

Serves 4–6

My late mum used to make this for my sister, as it was one of her favourite dishes for the Muslim celebration of Eid. Anything that my sister likes I tend to go against! I preferred my mum to cook egg noodles in beef broth (see page 170) instead, so there would always be a debate among the family about which dish she should cook to complement her famous chicken rendang (see page 109). I simply hated it if my sister won! I can only eat this dish once a day, as I find the fishy smell a bit overpowering, but my sister can eat bowlfuls of it without complaint. This particular type of *laksa* is very well known in Penang, so I just had to include it in the book. It even got voted in the Top 10 dishes of the world on CNN's website. It's infused with aromatic ginger flower and Vietnamese coriander (*laksa* leaves) – if you can't get hold of these from oriental stores, you can replace the ginger flower with lemongrass and the laksa leaves with basil. It won't be as good as the original but will still be delicious. I use ready-made udon rice noodles, which can be bought in Chinese grocers.

----

1 Blitz the spice paste ingredients in a food processor or with a hand blender until fine, and set aside.

2 Put the fish into a pan with 1.8 litres of water and bring to the boil. Scoop the fish into a bowl with a slotted spoon and use a fork to break the flesh into smaller pieces, removing any remaining bones. Keep the fish stock.

3 Add the spice paste to the stock, along with the Vietnamese coriander, ginger flower purée, tamarind, salt, sugar and fish pieces. Bring to the boil, then reduce the heat and simmer for 20 minutes.

4 Meanwhile blanch the noodles in boiling water for 1 minute, then drain and set aside.

5 To serve, put the noodles into small bowls and spoon over the broth. Garnish with the pineapple, cucumber, onion, chillies, mint and Vietnamese coriander leaves, and serve straight away.

Rice Vermicelli Fried Noodles

BIHUN GORENG

Malaysians are great at hospitality and making sure their guests are well fed and well looked after. I remember the time in the 1980s when I was growing up in the village of Kampung Sungai Nyior – the name means 'River of Coconuts Village' – and my cousins from Singapore came for a visit. They had to catch a train back home, which at the time was a whole day's journey. My mum was up at 5 a.m. to fry vermicelli noodles, then wrap them in banana leaves for my cousins to take on the train. This fried noodle dish is a favourite for a picnic or packed lunch, as it is easy to make. The vermicelli noodles are normally cooked with seafood and/or chicken, which you can add if you like, but I have made this version vegetarian.

----

1 Bring 3 litres of water to the boil in a large saucepan, then turn off the heat and blanch the vermicelli noodles for 2 minutes. Drain, transfer the noodles into a bowl of ice-cold water for 3 minutes, then drain again and set aside.

2 In a wok or a large frying pan, heat the oil over a high heat and sauté the garlic until golden brown. Add the chilli paste and fry for 1 minute, then add the noodles and both soy sauces and fry for 2 minutes, until well combined. Add the spinach and beansprouts and fry for 1 minute, or until the vegetables have wilted.

3 Add the spring onions and give another stir, then transfer to a large platter and serve straight away.

1 x 375g packet of rice vermicelli noodles
2 tablespoons vegetable oil
5 cloves of garlic, finely chopped
4 tablespoons chilli paste, ready-made from a jar or homemade (see page 204)
2 tablespoons sweet soy sauce
4 tablespoons light soy sauce
200g spinach, cut into 10cm strips
200g beansprouts
2 spring onions, thinly sliced diagonally into 2cm pieces

Serves 4

Hainanese Chicken Rice

NASI AYAM HAINAN

For the chicken and stock
6 boneless chicken breasts, about
  200–250g each
1 medium onion, quartered
2 spring onions, cut into 2.5cm slices
2.5cm fresh ginger
2 teaspoons fine sea salt
½ tablespoon sesame oil

For the rice
500g basmati or long-grain rice
8 cloves of garlic, lightly crushed
2.5cm fresh ginger, thinly sliced
2 tablespoons vegetable oil
1½ teaspoons fine sea salt
2 teaspoons sesame oil

For the garnish and to serve
2 baby lettuce or 1 iceberg lettuce,
  leaves picked
2 tomatoes, sliced into 1cm slices
300g cucumber, cut in half
  lengthways and cut into 1cm slices
Ginger soy sauce (see page 206)
Chilli and garlic dip (see page 207)

Serves 6–8

Famous in both Malaysia and Singapore, Hainanese chicken rice is a complete set meal, comprising sliced chicken, rice, soup, ginger soy sauce, chilli and garlic dip and crunchy vegetables, such as baby or iceberg lettuce, cucumber and tomato, on the side. Based on a recipe from the Hainan province of China, it is said to have travelled to Singapore and Malaysia with migrants from southern China, although like many dishes it has been adapted over time to suit local tastes. Singapore claims it as one of its national dishes, but it is just as popular in Malaysia at street food stalls, coffee shops and food courts.

This is my simpler version, using chicken breasts instead of the whole chicken. The chicken is poached until tender, then coated with sesame oil to enhance the flavour.

----

1 Put all the chicken and stock ingredients into a large pot with 4 litres of water. Bring to the boil, then cook for 10 minutes over a medium heat until the chicken is cooked through. Scoop out the chicken with a slotted spoon and place on a large plate or dish, covering it with aluminium foil to keep the heat in. Scoop out 1.15 litres of chicken stock and transfer to a separate pot. Continue simmering the remaining stock over a low heat for 15 minutes.

2 Add the rice, garlic, ginger, vegetable oil and salt to the 1.15 litres of stock. Bring to the boil, then reduce the heat to low and simmer for 8 minutes. Turn the heat off and add the sesame oil. Give it a good stir, then cover with aluminium foil to trap the steam in and set aside for 15 minutes.

3 To serve a complete Hainanese chicken rice, scoop out a small bowlful of rice on to a plate. Cut the chicken breast into 2cm-thick slices and arrange nicely on a plate with baby lettuce, tomato and cucumber. Pour 2 tablespoons of ginger soy sauce on to the chicken pieces. Serve the chilli and garlic dip in a small condiment saucer and the stock soup in a small bowl. Serve straight away.

Coconut Rice NASI LEMAK

Malaysians have this for breakfast but in quite small portions, nicely wrapped in a banana leaf for its aroma. It's typically served with hard-boiled eggs, fried anchovies, peanuts, cucumber slices and chilli sambal. When my mum sold it at the stall, she was up at five every morning to cook the rice. The smell of it was strong enough to wake me up at six to get ready for school. There are many good stalls in Kuala Lumpur that serve a very good nasi lemak, and Malaysians around the world can now enjoy World Nasi Lemak Day, which is celebrated on the first Sunday of every November, thanks to the 'Friedchillies' – the foodies of Malaysia!

----

1 Put all the ingredients apart from the condiments into a large deep saucepan with 1.1 litres of water and give a stir to mix thoroughly. Bring to the boil over a medium heat, then cover with a lid and simmer for 8 minutes, stirring once or twice. Turn the heat off, cover the saucepan with aluminium foil and leave for 15 minutes.

2 Transfer to a bowl and serve with the sambal and other condiments.

500g basmati rice, rinsed and
 soaked in water for 20 minutes
2.5cm fresh ginger, julienned
2 cardamom pods
5cm cinnamon stick
1 star anise
2 pandan leaves (or bay leaves)
 (optional)
1 stalk of lemongrass, bruised
250ml coconut milk
1½ teaspoons fine sea salt

For the condiments
Chilli sambal (see page 208)
100g dried anchovies, fried in 100ml
 vegetable oil until crispy
300g cucumber, peeled and cut into
 1cm slices
150g peanuts, dry-roasted and
 sprinkled with ½ tablespoon
 vegetable oil
4 hard-boiled eggs (see page 224)

Serves 4–6

1 Coconut Rice
2 Ginger Soy Sauce
3 Fried Anchovies
4 Peanuts
5 Chilli & Garlic Dip
6 Hainanese Chicken Rice
7 Perfect Hard-Boiled Eggs

Steamed Sticky Rice with Turmeric

PULUT KUNING

600g sticky rice
2 tablespoons ground turmeric
1 teaspoon black peppercorns
2 pandan leaves, each tied into a
  knot (or 2 bay leaves)
300ml coconut milk
1½ teaspoons fine sea salt

Serves 4

This sticky rice is served at various ceremonies in the Malay community, such as the birth of a child, an engagement, a birthday and many more. To celebrate the blessings received, rice is given as thanks to neighbours or sent to the mosque to be distributed to the villagers. The rice is soaked overnight, or for a minimum of four hours, to make the grains absorb the water, so that when it is cooked, it turns soft and fluffy. This type of rice contains a higher level of starch compared to normal rice, which is why it becomes sticky when cooked. Sticky rice is also milkier, looks whiter and is more fragrant.

----

1 Put the sticky rice into a bowl and add water to come 5cm above the level of the rice. Add the turmeric and peppercorns and give a good stir to mix well. Cover the bowl and let the rice soak for at least 4 hours – you can leave it overnight if you like.

2 Set up a steamer or put a rack into a wok or deep pan with a lid. Pour in 5cm of water and bring to the boil on a high heat.

3 Drain the rice and transfer into a round tray or cake tin that fits inside the steamer. Add the pandan knots and steam for 30 minutes, then transfer to a bowl, remove the pandan knots and add the coconut milk and salt. Mix thoroughly, then put the rice back into the tray or tin and steam for a further 15 minutes. Remove from the steamer again and give it a good stir.

4 Spoon into a bowl and serve with simple Malay chicken curry (see page 85), beef rendang (see page 96) or aromatic and rich lamb dry curry (see page 92).

Aromatic Beef Rice

NASI DAGING

I had heard about this rice dish so many times, but had never had a chance to try it until my sister-in-law cooked it for me a few years ago. Since then I've fallen in love with it. It is very similar to a biryani, and the beef blends well with the spices, making it aromatic and full of flavour. When my sister-in-law cooked it for me she was worried because she used the wrong type of rice. I was about to fly back to London the next day and she insisted on me trying it, and she ran out of basmati rice and used jasmine rice instead. It was a bit mushy and she was profusely apologetic. I get this all the time – people think because I am a chef I will be very fussy about what is served to me. I get fussy about what I cook for other people, and expect to be the best, but when people cook for me, I feel honoured. However, if I don't like it I will tell them the truth. This rice is nice served with a tamarind dip.

----

1 Heat a large deep saucepan over a medium heat and add 1.3 litres of water. Add the beef and the salt and bring to the boil, then reduce the heat to low and simmer for 30 minutes. Turn the heat off. Using a slotted spoon, scoop the pieces of beef into a bowl and set aside. Transfer the stock to another bowl. You will need 1.2 litres for the recipe.

2 Heat a second large deep saucepan over a medium heat. Add the ghee and sauté the raisins and cashew nuts for 30 seconds, then remove them with a slotted spoon and put them into a small bowl.

3 Add the onion to the ghee remaining in the saucepan and sauté until golden brown, then add the cinnamon, cardamoms, cloves, star anise and pandan knots and sauté for 1 minute, until fragrant.

4 Add the ground spice mix to the pan, then add the beef and cook for 2 minutes. Add the rice and evaporated milk, mix thoroughly to coat the rice with spices, then add the 1.2 litres of stock. Bring to the boil, then reduce the heat to low, cover with a lid and cook for 8 minutes, stirring once or twice. Turn the heat off, cover the saucepan with aluminium foil and leave for 15 minutes.

5 Sprinkle over the mint leaves, raisins and cashew nuts and give a good stir. Transfer to a bowl and serve straight away, with tamarind dip (see page 210).

400g beef topside, cut into chunks
2 teaspoons fine sea salt
150g ghee (or butter)
50g raisins
25g cashew nuts
1 large onion, diced
5cm cinnamon stick
4 green cardamom pods
4 cloves
1 star anise
2 pandan leaves, tied into a knot
 (or 4 bay leaves)
5 tablespoons ground spice mix for
 aromatic beef rice and rich lamb
 curry (see page 210), mixed with
 a dash of water
500g basmati rice, washed and
 soaked in cold water for 20 minutes,
 then drained
100ml evaporated milk
4 sprigs of mint, leaves picked

Serves 4–6

Herbal Rice NASI ULAM

This rice dish is full of fragrant herbs and is served cold as a salad. The original recipe has more herbs in it, but some of them are obviously difficult to find outside Malaysia. To make this a vegetarian dish, leave out the salted fish and add finely chopped fried spongy tofu, well seasoned with salt.

----

1 Heat a medium frying pan over a medium heat, then add the oil and fry the shallots until crisp and golden brown. Scoop out with a slotted spoon and dab with kitchen paper to remove excess oil.

2 Put the cooked rice, black and white peppers and salted fish into a large bowl and mix thoroughly (I recommend using your hands). Add the *kerisik*, salt and all the herbs and mix in well. Garnish with the fried shallots and serve straight away.

3 tablespoons vegetable oil
2 shallots, thinly sliced
1100g cooked basmati or long-grain rice (see page 144)
1 teaspoon coarsely ground black pepper
1 teaspoon ground white pepper
80g salted fish, lightly fried in a little oil, then cooled and pounded with a pestle and mortar
5 tablespoons kerisik (roasted coconut, see page 212)
2 teaspoons fine sea salt

For the herbs
2 tablespoons ginger flower purée (or lemongrass purée)
4 tablespoons finely chopped fresh mint leaves
4 tablespoons finely chopped fresh coriander
6 tablespoons finely chopped watercress (or pennywort)
4 tablespoons finely chopped lemongrass (use bottom half only)
4 tablespoons finely chopped Vietnamese coriander leaves (or mint or basil)
2 tablespoons finely chopped kaffir lime leaves (or lime rind)
4 tablespoons finely chopped Thai basil leaves (or regular basil)
2.5cm fresh ginger, finely chopped

Serves 4–6

Vegetable Egg Fried Rice NASI GORENG SAYUR

There are many types of egg fried rice and this is a vegetarian version. You can add different vegetables to this quick and simple recipe. It works well with leftover roasted vegetables.

----

1 Heat a wok or a large frying pan over a high heat. Add the oil and fry the garlic and ginger until fragrant and golden brown. Add the pak choy and mixed vegetables and cook for 1 minute, until the vegetables have wilted.

2 Scoop the vegetables to one side of the pan, then drizzle in a little oil. Crack in the egg and let it scramble, then mix thoroughly with the vegetables. Add the rice and the mushroom and soy sauces and fry for 2 minutes. Turn the heat off, add the white pepper, sesame oil and spring onion, and give another stir. Transfer to a platter and serve immediately.

2 tablespoons vegetable oil, plus extra for scrambling the egg
3 cloves of garlic, finely chopped
2.5cm fresh ginger, finely chopped
150g pak choy, cut into 2.5cm wide strips
150g mixed vegetables (green peas, sweetcorn and carrots)
1 egg
400g cooked basmati or long-grain rice (see page 144)
1 tablespoon mushroom sauce or vegetarian oyster sauce
3 tablespoons light soy sauce
½ teaspoon ground white pepper
1 teaspoon sesame oil
1 spring onion, cut into 0.5cm slices

Serves 2–3

Anchovy Egg-fried Rice

NASI GORENG IKAN BILIS

4 tablespoons vegetable oil, plus
  extra for scrambling the egg
30g dried anchovies
3 cloves of garlic, finely chopped
½ a medium onion, diced
1 tablespoon chilli paste, ready-
  made from a jar or homemade
  (see page 204)
300g boiled rice
1½ tablespoons sweet soy sauce
2 tablespoons light soy sauce
½ a carrot, peeled and diced
2 tablespoons frozen peas
1 egg, beaten
A pinch of white pepper

Serves 2–3

My YouTube video for this simple recipe has been viewed over 100,000 times – and hopefully more people will see it after reading this! The recipe works well if you have any leftover rice that would otherwise go to waste. You can add chicken, prawns or tofu, but for this recipe I want to celebrate my childhood memories of having this cooked by my late mum. She would only add anchovies. Dried anchovies are a kitchen cupboard essential for every Malaysian household; a good source of iron and omega-3, they also work well as a seasoning ingredient, like shrimp paste and fish sauce.

----

1 Heat a wok or a large frying pan over a medium heat. Add the oil and fry the anchovies for 1–2 minutes, until crisp, then scoop out and dab with kitchen paper.

2 Using the oil remaining in the pan, fry the garlic and onion until fragrant and golden brown. Add the chilli paste and fry for 30 seconds, then add the rice, both soy sauces, the carrot and the frozen peas. Mix well, then fry for 2 minutes, until the sauce is well mixed into the rice.

3 Push all the ingredients to one side of the wok, then drizzle in a little oil and crack in the egg. Let it scramble, then stir it into the rice and give it all a good mix. Add the anchovies and a pinch of white pepper and mix well, then scoop on to a platter and serve immediately.

Egg Fried Rice in Omelette Parcel

NASI BUNGKUS PATTAYA

2 tablespoons vegetable oil, plus
 extra for scrambling the egg
1 medium onion, diced
4 cloves of garlic, finely chopped
200g boneless chicken breasts, diced
1 egg
2 tablespoons oyster sauce
2 tablespoons light soy sauce
500g boiled rice (see page 144)
100g mixed vegetables (carrots,
 peas, green beans, sweetcorn)
1 teaspoon fine sea salt
½ teaspoon ground white pepper

For the wraps
4 eggs
Fine sea salt
2 tablespoons vegetable oil

Serves 4

**This is a Malaysian dish, but Pattaya is the name of a small town
in southern Thailand. No one is actually sure how the name came
about, and in Indonesia it is known as *nasi goreng amlop* – for the
'envelope'. The egg fried rice is wrapped in an omelette like an
envelope, so you have to get the omelette as thin as you can. It is
one of the most popular dishes at Malaysian food courts.**

**It makes a quick family lunch or midweek meal, and works well
made with leftover rice.**

----

1 Heat a wok or a large frying pan over a high heat. Add the oil and
sauté the onion and garlic until fragrant and golden brown. Add the
chicken and sauté for 2 minutes, to seal.

2 Scoop the chicken to one side of the wok or pan, then drizzle in a little
oil, crack in the egg, let it scramble, then mix with the chicken. Add the
oyster and soy sauces, rice, vegetables and salt and give a good stir.
Cook for 2 minutes, then turn off the heat and sprinkle with the white
pepper. Transfer to a bowl.

3 Beat one egg in a bowl and add a pinch of salt. Heat a large frying
pan, add ½ tablespoon of oil and pour in the beaten egg to create
a thin layer of omelette. Fry for 1–2 minutes, until cooked and turning
crispy golden brown. Gently remove from the pan and place on a flat
surface, ready for wrapping. Repeat with the rest of the eggs to make
4 omelettes.

4 Divide the fried rice into 4 portions. Place a portion on one of the
omelettes, then gently wrap like a parcel and flip over so the join is
underneath. This will prevent the parcel from opening up. Repeat with
the remaining fried rice and wraps, and serve straight away.

Mamak Fried Noodles

MEE GORENG MAMAK

Mamak noodles are very rich in flavour. When you go to a Mamak stall, they will sell three main dishes: *mee goreng mamak*, *rojak pasembor* and *mee rebus*. The ingredients for all three are very similar. The sauce is thickened with puréed sweet potato, which is rich in flavour. The tingling taste of vinegar is added for a light sharp sour taste. If you have the opportunity to visit Georgetown in Penang, go to the Mamak stall called Ais Tingkap at Tamil Street, just opposite Chowrasta Fresh Market – it serves prawn fritters, *air serbat* (coconut juice with rose syrup, basil seeds and coconut flesh), and these noodles, fried by a Mamak in his eighties. The fritters are added to give a texture to the noodles, but you can do without.

----

1 Bring 2.5 litres of water to the boil in a large deep saucepan. Add the noodles and cook for 10 minutes, until soft, then drain and set aside.

2 Heat a large wok or frying pan over a high heat, then add the oil and sauté the garlic until fragrant. Add the chicken and squid and cook for 2 minutes.

3 Now add the chilli paste and fry for 1 minute, then add the noodles, both soy sauces, tomato ketchup, vinegar and sweet potato purée and fry for another 2 minutes.

4 Scoop the noodles to one side of the wok or frying pan. Drizzle in a little oil, crack in the eggs, let them scramble, then mix them with the noodles. Add the beansprouts, potatoes, spinach and the cooked fritters. Fry until the vegetables wilt, then transfer to a platter and serve immediately, with the lime wedges.

300g dried egg noodles
3 tablespoons vegetable oil, plus extra for scrambling the eggs
5 cloves of garlic, finely chopped
300g boneless chicken breasts, thinly sliced
200g squid, scored and cut into pieces
3 tablespoons chilli paste, ready-made from a jar or homemade (see page 204)
4 tablespoons dark soy sauce
4 tablespoons light soy sauce
2 tablespoons tomato ketchup
1½ tablespoons white vinegar
75g sweet potato, boiled and puréed with a dash of water
2 eggs
200g beansprouts
150g potatoes, boiled and cut into chunks
100g spinach, cut into 10cm strips
6 fritters (see page 221), cut into small chunks (optional)
1 lime, cut into 4 wedges

Serves 4

Noodles in Soy Sauce with Seafood

MEE KICAP

1 tablespoon vegetable oil
3 cloves of garlic, finely chopped
2.5cm fresh ginger, finely chopped
100g raw mussels, in their shells
100g raw king prawns, peeled
100g squid, scored and cut into small
  pieces
2 tablespoons sweet soy sauce
1 tablespoon dark soy sauce
1 tablespoon oyster sauce
10g dried anchovies, soaked in
  water for 5 minutes and pounded
  (optional)
200g egg noodles, soaked in hot
  water for 5 minutes
50g pak choy
50g beansprouts
½ teaspoon ground white pepper
½ teaspoon sesame oil

Serves 2-3

Like many dishes in Malaysia, *mee kicap* has a strong 'fan base', just like *char kuey teow* (page 146). It's one of those dishes that I sometimes crave when I'm away from Malaysia. It's particularly famous in Ipoh, another great street-food city, towards the centre of Peninsular Malaysia. It has similar ingredients to Penang's famous *char kuey teow*, but uses egg noodles (instead of rice ones) and more soy sauce, making it 'wetter' and with a delicious balance of sweet and salty. I love it with seafood and oyster sauce, which give it a distinctively summery flavour. You can also make it a vegetarian dish if you like, by using a vegetarian oyster sauce and various kinds of tofu instead of seafood. Quick and easy to make.

----

1 Heat the oil in a frying pan over a medium heat and sauté the garlic and ginger until fragrant. Add the mussels, prawns and squid, discarding any mussels that are open and do not close when tapped. Cook for 2 minutes, then scoop the prawns and squid (but not the mussels) into a bowl and set aside. This is to prevent the seafood getting overcooked.

2 Add both soy sauces, the oyster sauce and the anchovies, along with 200ml of water, and simmer the mussels on a low heat for 5 minutes to reduce the sauce. Add the egg noodles, pak choy, beansprouts, white pepper and sesame oil and cook for 2 minutes, then put back the prawns and squid. Remove and discard any unopened mussels. Give another stir and turn the heat off, then transfer to small bowls and serve straight away.

Ipoh Curry Noodle Sauce MEE KARI IPOH

This is another famous dish from Ipoh (see also *mee kicap*, page 166). It's like noodle mania in this central Malaysian city, with its burgeoning and innovative food scene. There are all sorts of different styles of noodle dishes, but this is my take on an Ipoh curry noodle soup. Just like Malaysian cuisine as a whole, it's a wonderful concoction of different styles, ingredients and flavours, from spicy curry to mild soy sauces. It's Malaysia, in a bowl.

----

1 Purée all the paste ingredients in a food processor until smooth.

2 Put a large deep saucepan on a medium heat and add 1.75 litres of water. Add the chicken, anchovies, salt, cinnamon, star anise, cardamom pods and cloves and bring to the boil, then reduce the heat to low and simmer for 30 minutes. Turn off the heat.

3 In a separate saucepan, bring 2 litres of water to the boil over a medium heat. Add the egg noodles and cook for 6–8 minutes, or until the noodles are soft. Drain, rinse with cold water and set aside.

4 Heat a medium frying pan over a medium heat. Add the oil and sauté the paste for 2 minutes, until fragrant. Add the curry leaves and fry for a further minute, then add the paste to the chicken and anchovy stock. Turn the heat back on and bring to the boil. Add the coconut milk and tofu, then turn the heat to low and simmer for 5 minutes.

5 Add the noodles and beansprouts and cook for 1 minute. Garnish with chilli, fried shallots, mint leaves, lime wedges and hard-boiled eggs and serve straight away.

400g boneless chicken thigh pieces
25g dried anchovies (optional)
2 teaspoons fine sea salt
5cm cinnamon stick
2 star anise
4 cardamom pods
4 cloves
500g egg noodles
6 tablespoons vegetable oil
2 sprigs of curry leaves, leaves picked (or 3 bay leaves)
200ml coconut milk
8 pieces of ready-made fried spongy tofu, each cut into 4
100g beansprouts

For the paste
3 shallots
4 cloves of garlic
5cm fresh turmeric (or 2 teaspoons ground turmeric)
2.5cm fresh ginger
2.5cm fresh galangal (or extra ginger)
2 stalks of lemongrass
4 macadamia nuts
6 dried chillies, soaked in boiling water for 10 minutes
½ teaspoon shrimp paste, dry-toasted (or 1 tablespoon fish sauce)
1 tablespoon ground coriander
1 teaspoon ground cumin
1 teaspoon ground fennel

For the garnish
1 red chilli, cut into 0.5cm slices
3 tablespoons ready-made fried shallots
4 sprigs of mint, leaves picked
1 lime, cut into wedges
4 hard-boiled eggs, quartered (see page 224)

Serves 4–6

My Dad's Noodles

MEE REBUS PAK MUSA

Musa is my dad's name, and when we lived in Kampung Sungai Nyior, Butterworth, he was famous for his noodles. He could cook well, but only a few dishes. My parents tried to set up a stall thirty minutes away from the village, and it didn't do as well as expected, so they decided to bring the equipment home and sell the noodles outside our house. The pop-up stall became an instant hit with the villagers. My dad cooked the noodles and I helped to garnish. My mum was in charge of taking the money! I remember him telling me what I needed to garnish first. The garnish alone is like a work of art – first there were beef slices, then spring onions, chillies, hard-boiled eggs and finally fried shallots. Wonderful.

400g beef, cut into small chunks
2 teaspoons fine sea salt
300g dried egg noodles
2 tablespoons vegetable oil
1 medium onion, thinly sliced
5 cloves of garlic, thinly sliced
6 tablespoons chilli paste, ready-made from a jar or homemade (see page 204)
3 tablespoons tomato purée
1 teaspoon white sugar
30g dried shrimps, soaked in warm water for 10 minutes (optional)
50g roasted peanuts, crushed
200g beansprouts
100g pak choy

For the garnish
2 red chillies, thinly sliced
4 tablespoons ready-made fried shallots
1 spring onion, cut into 0.5cm slices
2 hard-boiled eggs, quartered (see page 224)

Serves 4

1 Heat a large deep saucepan over a medium heat and add 2 litres of water. Add the beef and salt and bring to the boil, then reduce the heat to low and simmer for 30 minutes. Turn off the heat.

2 In a separate saucepan, bring 2 litres of water to the boil over a medium heat. Add the egg noodles and cook for 6–8 minutes, or until soft. Drain, rinse with cold water and set aside.

3 Heat a medium frying pan over a medium heat. Add the oil and sauté the onion and garlic until fragrant and golden brown. Add the chilli paste, tomato purée, sugar, shrimps and peanuts. Cook for 3 minutes, then transfer to the pan of beef and stock. Give it a good mix and turn the heat back to medium. Bring to the boil, then add the noodles, beansprouts and pak choy. Cook for 2 minutes, until the vegetables have wilted.

4 Serve in small bowls, garnished with the chillies, fried shallots, spring onion and hard-boiled eggs, and serve straight away.

Chicken Fried Noodles

MEE GORENG AYAM

½ teaspoon fine sea salt
450g dried egg noodles
2 teaspoons sesame oil
2 tablespoons vegetable oil
3 cloves of garlic, finely chopped
½ a medium onion, thinly sliced
500g boneless chicken breasts, thinly
 sliced
6 tablespoons light soy sauce
4 tablespoons chilli paste, ready-
 made from a jar or homemade
 (see page 204)
2 tablespoons sweet soy sauce
300g pak choy, washed and trimmed
100g ready-made fried spongy tofu,
 cut in half
200g beansprouts

Serves 4–6

This is another of my favourite dishes made by my late mum. She cooked this every Sunday morning for breakfast after returning from the food market. I usually accompanied her to the market to help her carry the shopping, but as soon as she met her friends for their weekly gossip that was when I left her and carried it all back home. It may sound a bit heavy for some people, but this is one of the Malaysians' favourite breakfasts, along with our famous flatbread (see page 28) and coconut rice (see page 153). The noodles that are available back home are blanched and ready to cook, but for this recipe I use dried egg noodles, one of my essential kitchen cupboard ingredients. They are readily available in most supermarkets.

----

1 Bring 3 litres of water to the boil in a large pan and add the salt. Once boiling, add the noodles and boil for 8–10 minutes. Drain the noodles, then cool them in fresh cold water. Drain them again thoroughly and toss with the sesame oil. Put them aside.

2 Heat the vegetable oil in a wok or a large frying pan over a high heat. Add the garlic and onion and fry until fragrant and golden brown. Add the chicken and 1 tablespoon of light soy sauce, cook the chicken to seal it on all sides, then add the chilli paste. Cook for a further minute, then add the noodles, sweet soy sauce and the remaining light soy sauce. Continue frying for a further 2 minutes.

3 Add the pak choy, tofu and beansprouts and stir continuously until the vegetables have wilted. Turn off the heat, scoop on to a large platter and serve straight away.

Malay Fried Noodles

KUEY TEOW BASAH MELAYU

There is a restaurant in Permatang Pauh, Butterworth, that serves very good *kuey teow basah melayu*. There are six chefs in the kitchen, all lined up with their woks amid flames and smoke, making the dish. You can imagine the intense atmosphere and the adrenalin rush these chefs have. This is what I keep shouting (in a nicer way) to my cookery class students: 'Get the flame into your wok to get that charred flavour on your noodles!' They all panic, and you can imagine the intense clacking noise they make as they hit their heavy ladles on my unfortunate metal woks. Most of the students end up red-faced after wokking their noodles but still manage to smile. As for me, I have a giggle before saying, 'Well done!'

----

1 Put the rice noodles into a large pan and cover with boiling water. Leave for 4 minutes, then drain and rinse under cold water.

2 In a medium saucepan, bring 500ml of water to the boil and blanch the prawns until they are pink and cooked. Remove the prawns from the pan, reserving the liquid, then shell them (keeping the shells) and set them aside. Blend the shells in a food processor with the reserved prawn cooking liquid, then pour through a sieve and set aside.

3 Heat the 2 tablespoons of oil in a wok or a large deep frying pan and sauté the garlic until fragrant and golden brown. Add the cockles or mussels and the chilli paste, fry for 1 minute, then add the oyster sauce, soy sauce, anchovies and prawn stock and bring to the boil. Add the noodles and cook for 2 minutes.

4 Scoop the noodles to one side of the wok or frying pan, then drizzle in the ½ tablespoon of oil and crack in the eggs. Let them scramble, then mix thoroughly with the noodles. Add the prawns, together with the beansprouts and the garlic chives, and cook until the vegetables have wilted.

5 Spoon on to a platter and serve straight away.

400g rice noodles, 10mm wide
600g raw king prawns, peeled
2 tablespoons vegetable oil, plus ½ tablespoon for scrambling the eggs
5 cloves of garlic, finely chopped
50g cockle or mussel meat
6 tablespoons chilli paste, ready-made from a jar or homemade (see page 204)
8 tablespoons oyster sauce
4 tablespoons light soy sauce
30g dried anchovies, soaked in water for 5 minutes, then drained and pounded in a pestle and mortar until fine
2 eggs
200g beansprouts
50g Chinese garlic chives (or spring onions), cut into 2.5cm pieces

----

Serves 4–6

Puddings & Drinks

Fresh Mango, Honey & Coconut

MANGGA, MADU & KELAPA

Mangoes are a favourite dessert for Malaysians, and most village houses have mango trees growing in their front yard. I love the smooth and delicate texture of ripe mango. This is a quick refreshing dish that works well with honey, coconut and cinnamon. I use desiccated coconut that I've toasted but you can also use coconut flakes. The dish can be eaten as it is or served with vanilla ice cream or sticky rice (see page 144).

----

1 Place the mango on a serving plate and drizzle the honey on top, then sprinkle over the coconut and cinnamon. Serve with vanilla ice cream or sticky rice.

2 ripe mangoes, peeled and cut into strips
4 tablespoons clear honey
20g desiccated coconut, lightly toasted until golden brown (or 4 teaspoons coconut flakes)
¼ teaspoon ground cinnamon

Serves 2–3

Pandan Custard & Sticky Rice Layered Sweet SERI MUKA

300g sticky rice, soaked in water for
 4 hours
650ml coconut milk
1 teaspoon fine sea salt
4 medium eggs
200g white sugar
½ tablespoon pandan extract (see
 right, or 2 teaspoons vanilla extract)
3 tablespoons cornflour
3 tablespoons plain flour

Serves 4–6

I introduced this dessert at Ning and it didn't do well with the customers at the beginning, because of its colour; however, once I'd explained that the colour was due to the nutty and aromatic pandan extract, they tried and loved it and it's become a restaurant favourite. If you can't find pandan extract, use vanilla extract and add green food colouring. In the village where I grew up, there was a lady called Makcik Kiah who was well known for selling this. Hers was beautifully made, with the juice extracted fresh from the pandan leaves. It can be kept in the fridge for a week – to reheat, just steam again for 8 minutes. I've used a bottled pandan extract here, but if you want to make your own, using the leaves, cut 5 leaves into small pieces and blend with 200ml of water. Strain out the juice and use 100ml of juice – you can add the pulp to the water in the steamer if you like, for the aroma. If you are using fresh juice, reduce the coconut milk for the custard layer by 50ml.

----

1 Set up a steamer or put a rack into a wok or deep pan with a lid. Pour in 5cm of water and bring to the boil on a medium heat.

2 Put the sticky rice into a 23cm round cake tin, about 6cm high or higher, place in the steamer, and steam for 30 minutes. Set aside to rest for 5 minutes, then add 200ml of the coconut milk and the salt and press the steamed rice to make it level. Steam again for a further 10 minutes.

3 For the custard layer, whisk the eggs and sugar in a bowl until the sugar has dissolved. Add the pandan extract (or vanilla extract, if you can't find pandan) and the remaining coconut milk, and mix well. Sift in the flours and whisk until well combined.

4 Pour the mixture on top of the steamed sticky rice, smooth the top, and steam over a medium heat for 1 hour, leaving the steamer lid slightly open to prevent water from the steam from dropping on the custard layer. If this happens, though, and there is any water on the custard, dab it dry with kitchen paper.

5 Once cooked, cool completely, then slice and serve.

Photo also shows Pink Layered Pudding, overleaf

Pink Layered Pudding

KUIH LAPIS

100g tapioca flour
275g rice flour
300g white sugar
1 teaspoon fine sea salt
400ml coconut milk
4 tablespoons rose syrup or 6 drops
 of red colouring

Serves 4–6

Kuih means 'pudding' in Malay and refers to something sweet. You need a lot of patience to make this pudding, as each layer is steamed for 3 minutes to get the separate, beautiful colours. I admire Malaysian *makcik*, older ladies, for their patience in making this. These days people always want a short cut to making something beautiful like this. I've included this recipe to show my respect for my late mum and all the *makcik* who have not just passion but patience in cooking. I used to watch my mum making this, along with twenty other types of pudding, to be sold at her afternoon stall. If you can master this recipe you are one step closer to becoming a good chef. Let's put your patience to the test now!

----

1 In a large bowl, combine the tapioca flour, rice flour, sugar, salt and 800ml of water. Gradually add the coconut milk and mix well. Divide the batter into two portions, then add the rose syrup to one of the portions and mix well.

2 Set up a steamer or put a rack into a wok or deep pan with a lid. Pour in 5cm of water and bring to the boil on a high heat. Place a 23cm round cake tin in the middle of the steamer, then cover the steamer with a lid and steam for 5 minutes. This will help to prevent the batter from sticking to the tin.

3 Take off the lid and pour a ladleful of the plain batter into the tin, making sure the base is covered and that there is about 2mm thickness of batter. Steam for 3 minutes, then repeat with the rose batter. Repeat the process until all the batter is used up, then steam for a further 15 minutes to ensure the pudding is fully cooked.

4 Take the cake tin out of the steamer and let it cool down thoroughly, then invert and gently ease out the pudding. Cut into diamond shapes and serve at room temperature, with hot drinks.

Peanut & Sweetcorn Pancake APAM BALIK

Those who grew up in Penang in the 1980s will remember the *apam balik* stall that was located just by the bridge crossing at the jetty. There was always a long queue for these pancakes. They are made of plain and rice flours and coconut milk, with crushed peanuts, sugar and creamed sweetcorn fillings (you can buy the sweetcorn already creamed, in a tin). Every two weeks my family would make a visit to my grandmother in Gelugor, twenty minutes on the bus from Georgetown and only a short distance away from the Penang Bridge. Thankfully the village is still there, but my grandmother's beautifully crafted old wooden house has been demolished to make way for the bridge – something that really upset me, as I used to play in her courtyard. I remember the salty wind smell from the sea, and the sound of a marine patrol boat slicing through the waves at five in the morning. When we visited my grandmother, we would bring these pancakes with us but I ended up having most of them, eating the crispy part around the edge and leaving the fillings for the others to finish. They were not impressed. The rice flour is added to make the pancakes crisp. If you can't buy it, you can simply grind rice grains into a very fine powder, using a spice or coffee blender.

50g rice flour
150g plain flour
½ teaspoon bicarbonate of soda
½ teaspoon dried yeast
225ml coconut milk
1 egg
50g golden caster sugar
½ teaspoon fine sea salt

For the fillings
50g melted butter
50g brown sugar
50g peanuts, toasted and crushed
6 tablespoons creamed sweetcorn

Makes 6–8 pancakes

----

1 Sift the rice and plain flours into a large bowl and add the bicarbonate of soda, yeast, coconut milk, egg, sugar, salt and 225ml of water. Whisk until smooth, then cover the bowl with clingfilm and leave for 1 hour at room temperature.

2 Heat a heavy-based small frying pan over a low heat and grease it with 1 teaspoon of melted butter. Pour in a small ladle of the batter and use the back of the ladle to spread it evenly over the pan, out to the edges. Cook for 1 minute, sprinkling with 1 teaspoon of brown sugar per pancake while the batter is still runny.

3 Cover the pan with a lid and cook for 2 minutes, then take the lid off and check that the batter is firm. If it is, sprinkle over some crushed peanuts and pour on 1 tablespoon of creamed sweetcorn. Fold the pancake in half with a palette knife and take it out of the pan.

4 Repeat with the remaining batter and filling, greasing the pan again before you make each pancake. Serve straight away.

Sticky Rice Balls

ONDE ONDE BUAH MELAKA

This sweet Nyonya dessert is a favourite with Malaysians and is easy to make. The sweet balls have three different textures – crispy on the outside from the desiccated coconut, chewy in the middle from the sticky rice flour, and a runny liquid centre from the melted sugar. The best way to eat these is to put the whole ball into your mouth and bite into it so that you feel the melted sugar pop in your mouth.

----

4 pandan leaves (or 1 tablespoon
  ready-made pandan extract, see
  page 239, or 2 teaspoons vanilla
  extract with green food colouring)
350g sticky rice flour
100ml coconut milk
1 teaspoon fine sea salt
200g dark coconut sugar, cut into
  1cm cubes
200g fine desiccated coconut

Makes 40

1 Roughly cut the pandan leaves into small pieces and blitz in a blender with 200ml of water. Strain through a fine sieve over a bowl to remove the pulp, while retaining the juice. You will need 100ml of juice.

2 Put the sticky rice flour, pandan leaf juice (or pandan or vanilla extract), coconut milk and ½ teaspoon of salt into a bowl with 125ml water and mix to create a soft dough. If the dough sticks to your fingers, sprinkle it with a little rice flour. Form the dough into small balls about 2.5cm in diameter.

3 Gently push your finger into the centre of each ball to create a space for a sugar cube to fit. Place a cube in the space, then cover with the dough to make a ball again. Put aside and repeat the process with the rest of the dough.

4 Mix the desiccated coconut with the remaining ½ teaspoon of salt and sprinkle on a flat tray.

5 Bring 2 litres of water to the boil in a large pan, then reduce the heat to medium and carefully drop the balls into the hot water. When they change colour and start to float, leave them for 1 more minute, then scoop them out, drop them on to the tray of desiccated coconut, and coat well.

6 Allow to rest for 10 minutes before eating, as the melted sugar filling will be hot.

Rice & Coconut Steamed Cake

PUTU BULUH

8 pieces of banana leaf (or
 aluminium foil), 10 × 30cm
½ teaspoon fine sea salt
200g rice flour
100g desiccated coconut
50g molasses sugar

- - - - - - - - - - - - - -

Makes 8 pieces

**This is one of my favourite sweets – I always used to buy it when
I visited the night markets in Malaysia. *Buluh* means 'bamboo'
in Malay, and the cake is steamed inside bamboo stalks about
10cm long with open ends. For this recipe I have invented an
alternative, using a banana leaf tied with string to make a
cylinder shape. I am very pleased with the results! You can also
use a metal or plastic round mould with open ends, if you have one.**

- - - - - - - - - - - - - -

1 Clean the banana leaves, if using, then soften them by placing them
on a low flame or over steam from a kettle for a few seconds.

2 Put the salt into a large bowl with 150ml lukewarm water and
mix thoroughly. Add the rice flour bit by bit, to form a dough. Press
the dough through the holes in a medium-holed sieve to create a
breadcrumb-like texture. Add the desiccated coconut to the mixture
and mix well.

3 Set up a steamer or put a rack into a wok or deep pan with a lid.
Pour in 5cm of water and bring to the boil on a high heat.

4 To make a banana leaf mould, roll a leaf (or the aluminium foil) into
a cylinder shape about 4cm in diameter. Tie a piece of string around
the mould to secure it. Half fill the mould with the coconut mixture, then
create a hole in the middle and add 1 teaspoon of sugar. Now fill the
other half of the mould, pressing the mixture in gently, not too hard,
otherwise it will be too compact. The mixture will absorb the moisture
from the steam.

5 Repeat with the rest of the banana leaves and the remaining
mixture. Place the rolls in the steamer and steam for 10 minutes.

6 Remove the banana leaf moulds and serve immediately.

Rice & Coconut Sweet Pancake

APAM LENGGANG

Lenggang describes the movement you have to make with the wok or pan when making this. Often sold in morning fresh markets and served for breakfast, it is nice to have with Malaysian coffee 'O', which means coffee with sugar but without milk. The rice flour gives a crispy texture around the edge of the pancake.

----

1 Put the rice and plain flours, yeast, sugar and coconut milk into a bowl and add 200ml of water. Whisk until the batter is mixed well, then strain it into another bowl, cover with clingfilm and set aside for 1 hour.

2 Get a 20–25cm frying pan really hot and grease it with a bit of the oil or butter. Scoop out 1 ladleful of the batter and pour it into the hot pan in one go. As soon as the batter hits the pan, tip the pan so it will spread and create a thin layer around the edge.

3 It should only take 1 minute or so for the thin batter around the edge to begin turning turn crispy golden brown. Fold it over, then scoop it out of the pan. Repeat with the remaining batter. Best served warm.

150g rice flour
50g plain flour
1 teaspoon dried yeast
6 tablespoons white sugar
200ml coconut milk
2 tablespoons vegetable oil or butter,
 for greasing

Makes 10

Tropical Fruit Salad SALAD BUAH

This easy fruit salad is a favourite at my dinner parties. It is quick and simple and can be prepared ahead and kept in the fridge. If I'm in Malaysia I use fresh lychees, but if you can't get fresh ones, use the ones from a tin. Pomegranates are grown in Malaysia – they are called *delima*, which means rubies, because of their seeds, which look like precious stones. If you can't get lychee juice, use orange juice instead. Any leftover fruit salad can be put into a blender and turned into a smoothie, putting it through a sieve if you like, to remove any unblended pomegranate seeds.

\--------------

1 semi-ripe mango, diced
200g diced fresh pineapple
10 lychees
4 kiwi fruit, quartered
Seeds from 1 pomegranate
10 mint leaves
½ teaspoon ground cinnamon
1 star anise
500ml lychee juice

\--------------

Serves 4

1 Place all the ingredients in a large bowl and give them a good stir to mix in the cinnamon powder thoroughly.

2 Chill in the fridge for 20 minutes before serving.

Sweet Mung Bean Porridge BUBUR KACANG

400g dried mung beans, soaked for
  4 hours or overnight
1 pandan leaf, tied into a knot
  (optional)
50g sago
100g dark coconut sugar, finely
  chopped
200g molasses sugar
400ml coconut milk
1 teaspoon fine sea salt

Serves 6–8

This warm sweet porridge reminds most Malaysians of the 'cold' monsoon season, when they are stuck at home enjoying it. The porridge is served with white bread or sometimes with light crackers for dipping. The beans need to be soaked for at least 4 hours, but you can plan ahead by soaking them overnight. If you don't have dark coconut sugar, you can use more of the molasses sugar.

----

1 Bring 2.5 litres of water to the boil over a medium heat, then add the mung beans and the pandan knot and cook for 20 minutes.

2 Meanwhile, bring 500ml of water to the boil in a medium saucepan. Add the sago and cook for 15 minutes, until translucent, stirring once or twice. Drain, then soak in cold water for 1 minute, drain again and transfer to a bowl.

3 Once the beans are cooked, add the dark coconut and molasses sugars and cook for 2 minutes, until the sugar has dissolved. Add the coconut milk and salt, bring to the boil, then add the sago, reduce the heat and cook for 5 minutes.

4 Serve immediately, with soft white bread or light crackers.

Rice Pudding with Dark Coconut Sugar Syrup SAGO GULA MELAKA

Traditionally this pudding is made with sago, but as it is not widely available here, I have used pudding rice instead.

----

1 Place the rice in a large saucepan and cover with water. Bring to the boil, turn down the heat and simmer for about 20 minutes, or until all the water has been absorbed.

2 Pour the coconut milk into the saucepan and simmer for another 15 minutes, until all of the milk has been absorbed. Take off the heat.

3 Put the dark coconut and molasses sugars and the pandan knot into a small saucepan and add 150ml of water. Bring to the boil over a medium heat, then reduce the heat and cook for 5 minutes, to reduce the quantity to half.

4 To serve, scoop the rice pudding into small bowls and pour over the sugar syrup.

100g short-grain pudding rice
50g dark coconut sugar
100g molasses sugar
1 pandan leaf, tied into a knot
  (optional)
600ml coconut milk
½ teaspoon fine sea salt

Serves 4–6

Soya Panna Cotta with Passion Fruit & Crushed Chocolate Cookies TAU FU FA

This is a dessert I made for my supper clubs in London. I used to serve it with orange and strawberry compote, but now, at Ning, I serve it with passion fruit. Originally the dessert was served just with sugar syrup, but passion fruit adds another flavour and the chocolate cookies give a different texture. I use ready-made sweetened soya milk from a carton, but the unsweetened kind is also fine to use.

750ml sweetened soya milk
2 tablespoons cornflour
8g agar agar or vegetable gel powder
50g caster sugar
¼ teaspoon salt
150g dark coconut sugar or molasses sugar
2.5cm fresh ginger, peeled and grated
8 chocolate cookies, crushed
4 passion fruit
8 physalis (Cape gooseberries), for garnishing (optional)

Makes 8

----

1 Divide the soya milk into two portions, 250ml and 750ml. Put the 250ml of soya milk into a bowl with the cornflour and stir until combined. Pour the mixture through a fine sieve and set aside.

2 Put the remaining 750ml of soya milk into a saucepan with the agar agar, caster sugar and salt and bring to the boil over a medium heat. Reduce the heat to low and cook until the agar agar has dissolved – this should take about 6–8 minutes.

3 Add the cornflour and soya milk mixture to the pan and cook for 2 minutes. Pour through a fine sieve, then divide between eight small bowls or cups. Leave to cool for 10 minutes, then transfer them to the fridge and chill for an hour.

4 To make the syrup, put the dark sugar and ginger into a saucepan with 400ml of water and bring to the boil, then reduce the heat and simmer for 5 minutes.

5 To serve, gently sprinkle some of the crushed cookies on top of each bowl, then scoop out the centre of the passion fruit and spoon on top. Garnish with physalis (if you have them) and pour the syrup over. Serve straight away.

Pandan Ice Cream AISKRIM PANDAN

Pandan extract is used in many Malaysian desserts for its green colour, nutty aroma and almost vanilla-like flavour. I launched my limited edition range of ice cream as a bit of a gimmick, to promote Malaysian cuisine and to test out the market. Of the five flavours I launched, pandan was the best-selling. So here's my 'secret' recipe! I like to serve it with crushed peanuts and a simple chocolate sauce.

1 litre extra-thick double cream
500ml full-fat milk
¼ teaspoon fine sea salt
12 egg yolks
300g white caster sugar
1 tablespoon thick pandan extract
  (see page 239)

For the topping (optional)
150g plain chocolate (minimum 50% cocoa)
100ml full-fat milk
60g ready-salted or unsalted roasted peanuts, crushed

Makes 2.25 litres

---

1 Put the cream, milk and salt into a deep saucepan and simmer on a low heat until at boiling point.

2 Beat the egg yolks and caster sugar in a bowl until thick. Gently pour half the cream and milk mixture on to the eggs and sugar, continuously whisking, then whisk in the remaining cream and milk. Transfer the whole mixture back to the saucepan and add the pandan extract. Bring to boiling point, continuously stirring to prevent it curdling. This should take 3–4 minutes.

3 Using a fine metal sieve, strain the mixture into a freezer-proof dish or bowl, or a loaf tin. Let it cool down for 15 minutes, then transfer to the freezer. After 45 minutes take it out of the freezer and churn, and continue doing this every 45 minutes for 2–3 hours.

4 To make the chocolate sauce, break the chocolate into small pieces and put them into a heatproof bowl. Add the milk and set over a saucepan of boiling water until the chocolate is melted and combined with the milk. Let it cool completely.

5 To serve, scoop the ice cream into bowls, pour over the chocolate sauce and sprinkle the crushed peanuts on top.

Sweet Potato & Banana in Coconut Milk

SERAWA PISANG DAN UBI KELEDEK

200g sweet potato, peeled and cut
 into 2cm dice
800ml coconut milk
100g white sugar
½ teaspoon salt
6 bananas, peeled and cut
 diagonally into 2cm slices

Serves 4

This is a warming winter dessert. Sweet potato and banana give a different texture to the creamy coconut. If you don't like coconut, you can use soya milk instead. You can also add tapioca if you like: boil 50g of tapioca pearls in 500ml of water for 15 minutes until translucent, then drain and stir into the dish.

----

1 In a saucepan, boil the potatoes with 500ml of water for 8 minutes, then drain and set aside. Rinse the pan and dry with kitchen paper.

2 Add the coconut milk, sugar and salt to the pan and bring to the boil over a medium heat. Reduce the heat to low, add the potatoes and banana slices and cook for 2–3 minutes. Turn the heat off and serve.

Banana Fritter Balls CUCUR KODOK PISANG

My mum introduced these as a dessert when she first visited my restaurant in 2006. She was so happy when I let her cook in my kitchen, and she was even happier when the orders for these, served with vanilla ice cream, kept coming in. None of my kitchen staff at that time could make the fritter balls as neat and round as hers. If you want to do it the Malaysian way, you have to drop the mixture gently into hot oil (be careful!) using your fingers. To do this, scoop up a round blob of mixture with your fingers and, using your thumb, gently push the mixture down and let it drop slowly into the oil, more or less intact as a ball. If you are not confident about this, use an ice cream scoop or a deep spoon instead. You can use over-ripe bananas, the ones whose skins have started to blacken – it's a great way of using them up.

1kg ripe bananas, peeled
4 tablespoons white sugar
140g plain flour
70g self-raising flour
½ teaspoon fine sea salt
700ml vegetable oil

Serves 3–4

----

1 Mash the bananas in a bowl until smooth and puréed, then add the sugar, both flours and the salt along with 2 tablespoons of water. Mix well.

2 Heat the oil in a deep saucepan over a medium heat. To check whether it is hot enough, drop in half a teaspoon of the mixture and if you see the oil bubbling away, then it's ready. If you have a thermometer, it should be between 180 and 200°C. Gently drop small blobs of mixture into the hot oil. Each one should expand to the size of a golf ball.

3 Deep-fry the balls for 3–4 minutes, until the colour changes to a rich dark brown. Remove with a slotted spoon and place on kitchen paper to drain away the excess oil. Serve with vanilla ice cream, if you like.

Malaysian 'Pulled' Sweet Tea TEH TARIK

This sweet tea is a favourite with Malaysians for breakfast and late supper. My daily breakfast before my dad took me to school was this tea and *nasi lemak bungkus,* coconut rice wrapped in a banana leaf. When the tea is poured (pulled) from one jug to another, it froths up. Reduce the amount of sugar if you don't like it too sweet. I notice that it is now common for Malaysians to order *teh tarik kurang manis*, which means tea with less sugar. Good for them.

----

3 builder's tea bags
500ml boiling water
1½ tablespoons sugar
2 tablespoons condensed milk

Makes 2 tall glasses

1 Put the teabags into a large jug and add the boiling water, then leave for 5 minutes for a strong brew.

2 Now add the sugar and condensed milk, and stir. Remove the tea bags.

3 To create a frothy top, get another jug and pour the tea from one jug to the other. The higher you pour the tea the frothier the top. Do this five or six times, then serve, in a tall glass.

Lemongrass & Honey Tea TEH SERAI DAN MADU

4 stalks of lemongrass, bruised
 and cut into 1cm slices
3 teaspoons honey

- - - - - - - - - - - - - -

Serves 2–3

I use a lot of lemongrass in my cooking and, in my demonstrations, I advise my audience not to waste the unused top part (only the white lower part of the lemongrass is used for cooking, as it is not fibrous like the top), as you can use it to make this tea. Freshly picked lemongrass should give juice, but the one that is sold in the supermarkets often turns dry and you won't get as much juice from it. Lemongrass is very citrusy and we use it a lot in Malaysian cooking. It is also an antioxidant. Use 6 stalks here if you are using just the top part of the lemongrass.

- - - - - - - - - - - - - -

1 Bring 500ml of water to the boil and pour into a teapot. Add the lemongrass and let it brew for 3 minutes.

2 Add the honey just before you drink the tea.

Rose Syrup Drink AIR SIRAP

This fragrant, floral drink is served at traditional Malay wedding receptions. When I was little, I remember watching how the rose syrup was prepared for the wedding of my neighbour's daughter. The syrup was prepared a day before the wedding, then, on the wedding day, they diluted it with water and ice before it was served. The volunteer chefs cooked the syrup with rose water, spices, pandan leaf, sugar and red colouring. The drink can also be prepared with coconut juice, or you can add condensed milk to turn it into a *sirap bandung*.

200g white sugar
1 tablespoon rose water
1 star anise
1 pandan leaf, tied into a knot
  (or 1 vanilla pod)
2.5cm cinnamon stick

- - - - - - - - - - - - - -

Serves 2–3

- - - - - - - - - - - - - -

1 To prepare the syrup, put all the ingredients into a saucepan with 300ml of water. Bring to the boil, then simmer for 5 minutes over a medium heat, until the quantity is reduced by half.

2 To prepare the drink, add 2 tablespoons of the syrup to every 200ml of cold water. Add some ice cubes and serve straight away.

Iced Fresh Lime Juice LIMAU AIS

This is a wonderful, refreshing drink made simply with fresh limes. Malaysian limes, *kasturi* or *calamansi*, are smaller, sweeter and more intense in flavour than European ones, so here I have added a little more sugar to compensate. At street food courts there are normally one or two drinks sellers who will serve the customers of all the other food stalls, and whom you therefore pay separately. This is a classic, popular drink to ask for, if you're not sure what to choose – and it makes a change from asking for canned soft drinks, as many shy tourists do. For this version, I've added soda water and mint leaves to make it fizzy and fresher.

2 tablespoons white sugar
3 limes
1 litre soda water
12 mint leaves
2 handfuls of ice

Makes 4 glasses

----

1 Dissolve the sugar in a bowl with a dash of boiling water. Squeeze the juice from the limes.

2 Mix all the ingredients together in a large jug and add the ice. Leave for 2 minutes, then pour into glasses and serve.

Condiments

Chilli Paste CILI KISAR

15g red dried chillies

Makes 8–10 tablespoons

Chilli paste made from dried chillies is sold widely in Malaysia. It is cheaper to use than fresh chillies. The common name for it is *cili boh* and it is packed in different sizes and weights. I prefer to use dried chilli paste in my cooking for its intense red colour, but it's important to choose the right chillies for the dish you are making (see page 228).

----

1 Soak the chillies in boiling water for 10 minutes, to soften them a bit. Once the chillies can easily be torn, they are ready. Drain them, then blitz them with a dash of water, using a hand blender to turn them into a paste.

2 It's ready to use straight away, but will keep in the refrigerator for at least 2 weeks.

Dark Chilli Sauce

SOS CILI

4 red chillies, deseeded and blended
 with a dash of water
2 tablespoons hoisin sauce
2 tablespoons white vinegar
2 tablespoons dark coconut sugar
 or molasses sugar
A pinch of fine sea salt

This is a quick chilli sauce that is served with crispy beancurd rolls with chicken (see page 37) and crunchy fried spring rolls (see page 33). It keeps for 2 weeks in the fridge.

----

1 Heat a saucepan over a medium heat and put in all the ingredients, along with 100ml of water.

2 Bring to the boil, then reduce the heat to low. Simmer for 5 minutes and serve.

Ginger Soy Sauce

SOS HALIA DAN KICAP

1 teaspoon grated fresh ginger
100ml light soy sauce
150ml chicken stock, strained
 to remove any fat
1 teaspoon sesame oil

1 Put all the ingredients into a bowl and stir well, then set aside for 10 minutes before serving.

Chilli & Vinegar Dip

SOS CILI DAN CUKA

This chilli dip is ideal with Hainanese chicken rice (see page 152) and crunchy fried spring rolls (see page 33). If you find it a bit too spicy, add more sugar and lime juice.

40g red chillies, deseeded
1.5cm fresh ginger
2 tablespoons brown sugar
2 tablespoons white vinegar
4 cloves of garlic
¼ teaspoon fine sea salt
1 tablespoon lime juice

1 Blitz all the ingredients in a food processor or with a hand blender until smooth.

2 Transfer to a bowl and refrigerate. It keeps for 2 weeks in the fridge.

Chilli & Garlic Dip

SOS CILI DAN BAWANG PUTIH

40g red chillies, deseeded and puréed
4 cloves of garlic
2.5cm fresh ginger
2 tablespoons lime juice
A pinch of fine sea salt
1½ tablespoons golden caster sugar

1 Using a hand blender, blitz the chillies, garlic and ginger until smooth, then transfer to a bowl.

2 Add the lime juice, salt and sugar, along with a dash of water, and give a good stir.

Chilli Sambal SAMBAL CILI

1 medium onion
3 cloves of garlic
1.5cm fresh ginger
6 tablespoons vegetable oil
8 tablespoons chilli paste, ready-
 made from a jar or homemade
 (see page 204)
2 tablespoons tamarind paste
 (or lemon or lime juice)
3 tablespoons dark coconut sugar
 or molasses sugar
1 teaspoon fine sea salt
½ teaspoon shrimp paste, dry-
 toasted (or fish sauce)

There are more than 400 different types of dried chillies and the smaller they are, the spicier they will be. I prefer to use dried chillies for two reasons: for the rich and dark red colour they give to a dish, and because they keep in your store cupboard for a long time. The traditional chilli *sambal* (sauce) actually takes hours to make. The longer you simmer, the milder it becomes. The heat will fade away, and all you can taste is the aftertaste. My version is quicker to prepare, but the most important thing is to get the oil to separate. This *sambal* can be eaten as a condiment for fried noodles, rice and coconut rice (see page 153) but if you are cooking it to serve with coconut rice, double the recipe.

----

1 Blitz together the onion, garlic and ginger until smooth, using a food processor or hand blender.

2 Heat a saucepan over a medium heat. Add the oil and sauté the puréed ingredients for 2 minutes. Add the chilli paste, tamarind, sugar, salt and shrimp paste, along with 100ml of water. Bring to the boil, then reduce the heat to low and simmer for 5 minutes.

3 This can be kept in the fridge for 2 weeks.

Tamarind Dip AIR ASAM

½ teaspoon shrimp paste, dry-
  toasted (or fish sauce)
4 tablespoons tamarind paste
  (or lemon or lime juice)
1 teaspoon white sugar
A pinch of fine sea salt
2 medium onions, diced
2 tomatoes, seeded and diced
2 red chillies, seeded and thinly
  sliced
4 bird's-eye chillies, thinly sliced
  (optional)
1 tablespoon lime juice

This is a quick and easy dip, combining sour, sweet and spicy flavours, which can be served with aromatic beef rice (see page 157). The acidic and sour tamarind paste tones down the chilli heat.

----

1 Put the shrimp paste, tamarind, sugar and salt into a bowl and mix with 100ml of lukewarm water.

2 Add the remaining ingredients, mix thoroughly, and set aside for 5 minutes before serving.

Ground Spice Mix

REMPAH RATUS UNTUK NASI DAGING

2 tablespoons coriander seeds
1 tablespoon cumin seeds
1 teaspoon fennel seeds
½ teaspoon ground nutmeg
6 green cardamom pods, pounded
  until fine
2 teaspoons black peppercorns
5cm cinnamon stick, broken into
  pieces
8 cloves
2 star anise, broken into pieces

I use this spice mix for Aromatic Beef Rice (see page 157) and Rich Lamb Curry (page 92). You can prepare this spice mix in advance and store it in an airtight container in the fridge, where it will keep for months.

----

1 Heat a frying pan over a low heat. Add all the spices and toast for 1 minute, until fragrant.

2 Use a spice grinder or coffee grinder to blitz the spices to a fine powder.

Ground Spice Mix for Meat

REMPAH RATUS UNTUK DAGING

This is the ground spice mix used for the meat curries, but you can also use this for a vegetable curry. In Malaysia there are different types of pre-packed ground spice mixes available, including my own brand, which I launched to encourage people in Britain to cook Malaysian curries. For this recipe, add less ground chilli if you prefer it less spicy, or add ground paprika as an alternative. If you have any of the spice mix left over, keep it in an airtight container. It will keep for a few weeks.

----

1 In a frying pan over a medium heat, dry-toast the coriander, cumin, fennel, cinnamon, star anise, cloves and cardamom for 1 minute, or until the aroma rises.

2 Use a spice grinder to grind the spices to a fine powder, then transfer to a bowl, add the turmeric and chilli, and give it a good stir.

2 tablespoons coriander seeds
2 teaspoons cumin seeds
2 teaspoons fennel seeds
1 cinnamon stick, broken into pieces
1 star anise, broken into pieces
2 cloves
2 cardamom pods
1 teaspoon ground turmeric
1 tablespoon ground chilli

Makes 5–6 tablespoons

Roasted Coconut KERISIK

200g creamed coconut block

Makes 6 tablespoons

The traditional way to make *kerisik* is by toasting the freshly grated coconut until brown and then pounding with a pestle and mortar. The coconut turns into a paste and becomes covered with a glaze, which is the coconut oil. I recommend that my cookery class students use a simpler method, using the creamed coconut block that comes in a small box and simmering it on a low heat. With this method you don't have to pound the coconut, as the creamed coconut melts and turns brown when simmered. The *kerisik* turns solid once it is cooled down completely, and lasts for a few weeks if you refrigerate it.

----

1 Unwrap the coconut block and cut it into smaller pieces. Heat a small frying pan on a low heat, then add the coconut and simmer for 10 minutes, stirring continuously.

2 Turn off the heat and set aside for 5 minutes before using.

Coconut Sambal SAMBAL KELAPA

This is a great condiment addition to a fresh crunchy salad. If you can't get fresh coconut, or haven't the time to grate it, you can use the dried desiccated coconut sold in packets, which is what I recommend for this recipe. The best technique for getting the right amount of moisture into the dried coconut is by steaming it. A traditional ingredient is *selom* leaves, which are not available outside Malaysia. As an alternative I use fresh mint leaves, which work well with the coconut.

----

1 Set up a steamer or put a rack into a wok or deep pan with a lid. Line the top with baking paper. Pour in 5cm of water and bring to the boil on a medium heat.

2 Steam the desiccated coconut for 10 minutes, until it becomes fluffy. Transfer to a bowl with all the remaining ingredients.

3 Gently mix everything together thoroughly, and serve straight away.

100g dried desiccated coconut
2 red chillies, deseeded and
 pounded
½ a shallot, pounded
10 mint leaves, finely chopped
1 tablespoon kerisik (roasted coconut,
 see page 212)
1 tablespoon lime juice
½ teaspoon fine sea salt

Serves 4

Spring Roll Pastry KULIT POPIAH

480g plain flour
1 teaspoon fine sea salt
2 egg whites
4 tablespoons white vinegar

Makes around 25–30 pieces

This pastry makes me think of a neighbour my family once had. She was known as Makcik Popiah, and I never got to know her proper name – that's what she was famous for, making *popiah* pastry. I saw her making it once, and she was quick. She rubbed a flat pan with the dough and used a skewer to lift off the cooked pastry – all within seconds. After she passed away, the business was taken over by her son. Many people think making this pastry is difficult, but it's easy once you get the hang of it, even though you may never be as fast as Makcik Popiah! It's fun to make, and you can really tell the difference in how rustic and original it tastes compared to the machine-made pastry you can buy in the supermarket. Obviously buying it is a lot easier, but if you really want to impress your guests, try making it yourself. The pastry may not be as smooth and perfectly shaped as the machine-made kind, but you can taste the difference. This pastry can be used to make Soft Spring Rolls (see page 34) and Fried Spring Rolls (see page 33).

----

1 Put the flour and salt into a large bowl and mix thoroughly. Mix the egg whites and vinegar in a small bowl with 300ml of water, then pour into the flour. Knead until well mixed – the dough should be sticky. Cover the bowl with clingfilm and leave to prove for 30 minutes, during which time the dough will become more elastic.

2 Set a flat pan (a roti pan or frying pan) on a very low heat. Use your hand to scoop up a handful of the sticky dough, then rub the pan with the dough to make a round shape, lifting up the dough instantly. Avoid your fingers touching the pan when rubbing the dough on the pan. Cook the pastry for 15 seconds, then scoop up using a flat spatula. Cover the cooked pastry with a damp cloth to keep it moist, then wipe the pan clean with kitchen roll. Repeat until the dough is used up, wiping the pan again each time.

Sweet Chilli Sambal (for Spring Rolls)

SAMBAL CILI POPIAH

This sauce can be served with either soft or crunchy fried spring rolls (see pages 34 and 33). The sauce is brushed on top of the spring rolls instead of being used for dipping.

----

1 Purée the onion and garlic until smooth, using a hand blender. Heat the oil over a medium heat in a medium saucepan and sauté the puréed onion and garlic until fragrant and golden brown. Add the rest of the ingredients, together with 200ml of water.

2 Bring to the boil, then reduce the heat to a simmer for 5 minutes. The sauce should thicken up enough to be easily brushed on to the spring rolls for serving.

1 medium onion
4 cloves of garlic
2 tablespoons vegetable oil
8 dried chillies, soaked in boiling
  water for 10 minutes, then puréed
2 tablespoons sweet soy sauce
2 tablespoons dark coconut sugar
  or molasses sugar
1 tablespoon tamarind paste
  (or lemon or lime juice)
1 teaspoon white vinegar
½ teaspoon fine sea salt

Makes 1 bowlful

Green Chilli Sambal SAMBAL CILI HIJAU

80g large green chillies, seeded
10g green bird's-eye chillies
1 shallot
1.5cm fresh ginger
3 cloves of garlic
15g dried anchovies, soaked in warm
  water for 10 minutes and drained
  (optional)
1½ tablespoons brown sugar
1½ teaspoons fine sea salt
1 tablespoon coconut oil
1 tablespoon lime juice

Serves 2–3

This *sambal* is originally from Padang island, Sumatra, in Indonesia, but it has been introduced into the Malaysian cuisine and there are now different versions of it available in Malaysia. The pounding method, using a pestle and mortar, works better here than using a food processor or hand blender. The sauce is best served with rice.

----

1 Using a pestle and mortar, pound all the ingredients except for the oil and the lime juice to a rough paste.

2 Heat a small saucepan over a medium heat. Add the oil and sauté the paste for 2 minutes. Turn off the heat and add the lime juice. Mix thoroughly and allow to completely cool, then refrigerate. Keeps for 4 weeks.

Quick Curry Sauce for Dipping

KUAH KARI RINGKAS

This is a simple recipe for a curry dip for beef murtabak (see page 32) or Malaysian flatbread (see page 28). You can add vegetables such as carrots, potatoes or fine beans, or just serve it as it is.

----

1 Heat a saucepan over a medium heat. Add the oil and sauté the shallot, garlic and ginger for 2 minutes, until fragrant and golden brown.

2 Add the curry mix, tamarind, salt and sugar and cook for 1 minute, then add the coconut milk, vegetables and 400ml of water. Bring to the boil, then reduce the heat, simmer for 2 minutes, and serve.

2 tablespoons vegetable oil
1 shallot, finely chopped
2 cloves of garlic, finely chopped
1.5cm fresh ginger, finely chopped
2 tablespoons ground spice mix for
  meat (see page 211), mixed with
  a dash of water
½ tablespoon tamarind paste
  (or lemon or lime juice)
½ teaspoon fine sea salt
½ teaspoon white sugar
1 tablespoon coconut milk
60g carrots, diced
20g fine beans, cut into 1cm pieces

Peanut Sauce KUAH KACANG

150g raw peanuts, blanched
8 tablespoons vegetable oil
1 stalk of lemongrass, bruised
2 tablespoons tamarind paste
 (or lemon or lime juice)
4 tablespoons dark coconut sugar
 or molasses sugar
2 teaspoons fine sea salt
3 tablespoons sweet soy sauce
4 tablespoons coconut milk

For the paste
3 stalks of lemongrass (use bottom
 half only)
5 cloves of garlic
5cm fresh ginger
2 shallots
12 dried chillies, soaked in hot water
 for 5 minutes

Serves 2–3

This used to be my secret recipe until I started teaching it in my cookery classes! Peanut sauce is best served as a dip with satay, or prawn fritters. The raw peanuts can be dry-roasted in a frying pan or in the oven, but before blitzing them in the food processor, make sure they have completely cooled down. This will help make them crunchy and not soft and 'stale'. If you are making this sauce for chicken satay (see page 24), double the recipe.

----

1 Heat a wok or a medium frying pan over a medium heat and dry-toast the peanuts for 5 minutes, until charred. Cool down completely, then blitz in a food processor or with a hand blender, leaving them slightly coarse-textured. Scoop into a bowl and set aside.

2 Purée all the paste ingredients until smooth, in a food processor or using a hand blender.

3 Heat a medium saucepan over a medium heat, and add the oil and lemongrass. Wait until the oil sizzles, then add the paste. Sauté for 2 minutes, then add the tamarind, sugar and salt and cook for a further 2 minutes, until the oil separates.

4 Next add the peanuts, soy sauce and coconut milk, along with 400ml of water. Bring to the boil, then reduce the heat to low and simmer for 5 minutes, until the sauce has thickened and produced a layer of oil at the top. Serve warm.

Savoury Mamak Fritters

CUCUR GORENG

These are the fritters to use in Mamak egg fried noodles (see page 165), and you can also eat them as a snack, with peanut or chilli sauce (see opposite and page 206).

----

1 Put all the ingredients apart from the frying oil into a bowl, add 150ml of water and mix well. Set aside for at least half an hour.

2 Heat the oil over a medium heat. Drop in the batter one spoonful at a time and fry for few minutes, until crisp and golden brown.

50g plain flour
50g rice flour
25g cornflour
½ teaspoon dried yeast
½ teaspoon white sugar
½ teaspoon fine sea salt
500ml vegetable oil, for frying

Nyonya Vegetable Pickle

ACHAR NYONYA

When it to comes to Malaysian pickles, I must say that the Nyonya kind are the best, partly due to the richness of the range of ingredients used. There is a good balance of vinegar and spiciness, and an array of beautiful textures and crunchiness from the vegetables and peanuts. You can keep this for up to 4 weeks in the fridge, but the longer you keep it, the more the vegetables will lose their crispness. Eat it as a condiment with rice.

---

1 Blitz the spice paste ingredients in a food processor. In a medium saucepan, heat the oil over a medium heat and sauté the spice paste for 2 minutes, until fragrant. Add the sugar and salt and cook for 1 minute, until the sugar has dissolved. Add the vinegar and give it a good mix, then turn the heat off and set aside.

2 To blanch the vegetables, bring 600ml of water to the boil in a saucepan and add the vinegar, sugar and salt. Add the vegetables (apart from the cucumber – don't blanch this, as it will lose its crunchiness) and blanch for 10 seconds, until slightly wilted. Scoop out with a slotted spoon and drain on kitchen paper.

3 Put the spice paste, the vegetables including the cucumber, the pineapple, peanuts, and sesame and coriander seeds into a glass bowl. Mix thoroughly, then transfer to a glass jar and refrigerate for 2 hours before serving.

3 tablespoons vegetable oil
100g white sugar
1½ teaspoons fine sea salt
150ml rice vinegar
100g pineapple, cut into 2cm thick wedges
150g peanuts, roasted and coarsely pounded
4 tablespoons sesame seeds (ideally 1 tablespoon black and 3 tablespoons white), roasted
2 tablespoons coriander seeds, roasted

For the spice paste
1 stalk of lemongrass (use bottom part only)
10 dried chillies, soaked in boiling water for 10 minutes
3 shallots
4 cloves of garlic
2.5cm fresh turmeric
2.5cm fresh galangal (or ginger)
4 macadamia nuts
1½ teaspoons shrimp paste, dry-toasted

For the blanching
200ml vinegar
2 tablespoons white sugar
1 teaspoon fine sea salt

For the vegetables
250g purple aubergines, cut into 5cm strips
300g white cabbage, cut into 2cm wide pieces
100g cauliflower, cut into small florets
100g carrots, peeled and cut into 5cm strips
100g fine green beans, cut into 5cm pieces
6 bird's-eye chillies
500g cucumber, peeled, deseeded and cut into 5cm long strips

Serves 4–6

Perfect Hard-boiled Eggs

TELUR REBUS

4 eggs
½ tablespoon white vinegar

This recipe tells you how to hard-boil eggs and get a solid but still bright yellowy-orange yolk. The eggs can be served as a condiment for coconut rice (see page 153) or prawn curry laksa (see page 149).

----

1 Put the eggs into a saucepan and add cold water to come 2.5cm above them. Add the vinegar and bring to the boil. (The vinegar is added to stop the egg spilling out if there is a crack.)

2 Time the eggs 8 minutes from when the water starts boiling. Scoop them out with a slotted spoon and rinse under cold water.

3 Peel the eggs and slice them with a cotton thread to get a nice cut. This is how it was done traditionally if you didn't have an egg slicer. Tie the thread to your kitchen drawer handle or ask someone to hold one end for you. You can slice the eggs into halves or quarters.

Onion Relish

JERUK BAWANG

2 tablespoons white sugar
4 tablespoons white vinegar
1 medium red onion, thinly sliced

This relish goes well with beef murtabak (see page 32).

----

1 Put the sugar into a bowl and add 200ml of warm water. Stir to dissolve the sugar, then add the vinegar and onion and mix well.

2 Refrigerate for 15 minutes before serving.

Yoghurt Dip

SOS YOGURT

Serve this dip with Malaysian Indian lentil patties (see page 42).

----

1 Mix all the ingredients in a bowl, adding a dash of water.

2 Refrigerate for 10 minutes before serving.

6 tablespoons yoghurt
3 sprigs of fresh mint, leaves picked
  and finely chopped
1 tomato, seeded and diced
100g cucumber, seeded, peeled and
  diced

Spiced Yoghurt Dip

SOS YOGURT BEREMPAH

Serve this dip with fried spiced chicken (see page 114).

----

1 Place yoghurt in a small serving bowl.

2 Sprinkle chilli flakes, cumin and mint leaves on top and ready to serve.

6 tablespoons yoghurt
½ teaspoon chilli flakes
1 teaspoon cumin seeds, coarsely
  pounded
1 tablespoon finely chopped mint
  leaves

WN GORENG

EOW GORENG

GORENG

3.00

NASI BUBUR

+

DAGING@AYAM

+

IKAN BILIS

RM4.50

LAKSA UTARA

LAKSAM

RM4.00

SO

RM

The Malaysian
Storecupboard

The Essentials

There are many specialist ingredients in authentic Malaysian cuisine, but if you have the following basics in your store cupboard you will be well on the way to creating the recipes in this book.

Here is my shopping list of essential ingredients, with explanations that will help you select and prepare them. Most of these basics will keep for a year or two in your cupboard or fridge, and they are the best ingredients to get you started with different types of Malaysian dishes. I hope, though, that you will get into Malaysian cooking so much that you will end up using them regularly, and extend your collection.

Tamarind
ASAM JAWA

This is a souring ingredient that balances out the spiciness of a dish. It comes in two forms, paste and pulp. I buy the pulp to use in my restaurant, as it is a lot cheaper, and once opened you can store it in an airtight container and keep it in the fridge for a long time. The pulp comes in a block, and to create the juice you need to soak it in water and press out the juice. As a general rule, I mix 100ml of water with ½ tablespoon of tamarind pulp to get tamarind juice. It's a bit more work, but a better and cheaper result. Alternatively, you can use the ready-made pastes that come in tubs or jars. These are more readily available in supermarkets and more convenient, as all you need to do is to scoop some out with a spoon. If you can't find tamarind, a souring agent such as lemon or lime juice can be used as an alternative.

Dried Chillies
CILI KERING

I get asked many times why I always use dried chillies in my cooking. Firstly, dried chillies keep longer in my store cupboard, and secondly, the colour of the finished dish is stronger, with a more intense crimson red colour than when you use fresh chillies (see page 238), which make a dish look pale as they contain moisture.

There are many types of dried chilli and you have to be careful in selecting the right ones. As I tell my cookery class students, the smaller chillies they are, the hotter they will be. Bite the tip of a chilli to check how spicy it is before using it in a recipe. If there is an immediate rush of heat, you know the chilli is spicy. If you can taste the heat only a couple of seconds after you bite it, then the chilli is not that spicy. Malaysian dried chillies are thin, long and wrinkly, and hard to find in the UK. Instead I use any big dried chillies that are more than 10cm long. If you can feel the heat on your fingers, rub them with lemon or lime juice and leave it on for 2 minutes before washing your hands with water.

Rice

BERAS

I use two types of rice in my recipes: basmati and jasmine. I prefer to serve jasmine rice with curries or stir-fries, as it absorbs the sauce nicely. When making a flavoured rice like coconut or tomato rice, I recommend using basmati, as it will be less mushy and will not overcook the way jasmine tends to when other ingredients are added. The long grain of basmati rice makes flavoured rice dry, light and fluffy. Ideally you should keep both types of rice in your kitchen cupboard. Most Malaysian village households keep rice in the *tempayan*, an earthenware crockpot like the one my late mum had. We also stored unripe mangoes in there to ripen them and give them a sweeter taste.

Shrimp Paste

BELACAN

This is not a favourite ingredient for many westerners because of its strong, pungent smell. It is made with shrimps dried under the sun, salted and pounded into a firm paste. The best shrimp paste comes from Pulau Aman, a small island about thirty minutes' drive from my home town of Butterworth, Penang, and fifteen minutes by boat. As it is the Malaysian equivalent of fish sauce, you can use this as a substitute if you can't find shrimp paste. It usually comes in a block, or sometimes in a tub. It is used to add flavour and is best dry-toasted in a frying pan before adding it to dishes. I toast the whole shrimp paste block at once, cutting it into thin slices, and when toasted, I keep it in an airtight container in the fridge. This saves having to toast it again and again, which is a good thing, as the smell may linger in your kitchen. To get rid of the smell, burn a small amount of old newspaper in a metal bowl – the smell of burnt paper will get rid of the strong smell of shrimp paste. (Please stay in the kitchen until you are sure the fire is out if you want to try this tip!)

Candlenuts

BUAH KERAS

These nuts are used in Nyonya cooking as a thickener and to enrich curries. The Malay word *keras*, meaning 'hard', refers to the texture, while the English 'candle' comes from the nuts' waxy and shiny look – they have a high oil content. Before using, the nuts are pounded with a pestle and mortar until fine. You can normally buy candlenuts from Chinese groceries. They are also known as *kemiri* nuts, and can be replaced with macadamia nuts if you can't find them.

Raw Peanuts

KACANG MENTAH

It's easy to buy peeled or blanched peanuts these days, but if you can't find any, you can dry-toast peanuts with their skins on, let them cool down slightly, then rub them with your fingers until you can feel the peanut skins peeling off. Then air them by lifting the tray up and down and blowing them until the skins come off the tray. This method is called *tampi*, and in my opinion is not the most hygienic way, but it's how it is done traditionally in family cooking. I once did this using an upright standing fan in the living room without thinking about what might happen next. The room was covered everywhere with peanut skins! My mum wasn't very pleased, and I had to clean up the whole mess before I could enjoy what she had cooked.

1 Fresh Turmeric
2 Raw Peanuts
3 Blanched Peanuts
4 Shrimp Paste
5 Coconut Milk
6 Tamarind Pulp
7 Fresh Tamarind
8 Kaffir Lime Leaves
9 Fresh Galangal
10 Fresh Coconut
11 Ginger
12 Desiccated Coconut
13 Lemongrass
14 Tamarind Paste
15 Curry Leaves
16 Ground White Pepper
17 Dark Coconut Sugar
18 Red Chillies
19 Dried Anchovies
20 Ground Turmeric
21 Garlic

4

3

5

9

10

11

12

16

17

15

21

20

Dried Noodles
MEE DAN BIHUN

Noodles come in different varieties, such as egg noodles, vermicelli, flat rice noodles and many more. Most Malaysians like to keep instant noodles in their store cupboard too – these come with a seasoning that contains MSG, and the noodles are often coated in a wax, which is not good for your health. I prefer to keep egg noodles and rice vermicelli in my cupboard. A 400g packet is enough for 4–6 people. Before using, you need to soak the noodles in hot water with the heat turned off – 8 minutes for egg noodles but only 4 minutes for rice vermicelli, otherwise they will get overcooked, ruining their texture. Run them under cold water to cool them down quickly and prevent the noodles from continuing to cook in the residual heat. This way they will not go soft when subsequently fried or added to a soup.

Creamed Coconut
KELAPA BEKU

This is my favourite form of coconut for keeping in my kitchen store cupboard. It is richer than coconut milk, an essential ingredient in Malaysian cooking. Cut the block into smaller chunks and keep any unused chunks in the fridge for another day. This is better than using tinned coconut milk because it avoids wastage, but if you prefer the milk, use what you need from the can and freeze any leftovers in ice-cube trays. One cube of frozen coconut milk should give you 15ml, which is the equivalent of 1 tablespoon. If you don't have coconut milk to hand, or prefer not to use it, you can replace it with fresh cow's milk, soya milk, or sometimes yoghurt, as in Indian cooking. I also use creamed coconut to make *kerisik* (roasted coconut, see page 212), as this is a quicker way to prepare it than the traditional method.

Cooking Oil
MINYAK MASAK

The oil I use in most of my cooking is standard vegetable oil, but you can also use sunflower, rapeseed or corn oil. I don't recommend olive oil, as the cooking temperature will not be high enough to fry your ingredients well and the flavour is too strong for some dishes. I normally keep at least 2 litres of cooking oil in my store cupboard. Most Malaysian cooking uses vegetable oil to fry the ingredients, but if you think there seems to be too much in some of my recipes, don't worry – I used that amount for a reason. You can always scoop out the excess oil after you finish cooking or when the oil starts to separate. My all-time favourite oil for cooking is coconut oil, but it is not cheap to use it every day. When I was young it was very cheap in Malaysia, but since then it has been overtaken by palm oil, which is cheaper, and sadly coconut oil is now hard to come by. Coconut oil has a lot of health benefits, though, and I highly recommend it for any of my recipes, if you can afford it.

Rice Vinegar
CUKA BERAS

This vinegar is made from fermented rice and is milder and less sharp compared to normal white vinegar. It is used in *achar* or pickles, and also in curries with a Eurasian influence, like my devil's curry (see page 105). If you don't have lime, lemon or tamarind to hand, you can use rice vinegar as an alternative.

Dried Anchovies
IKAN BILIS

The Malaysian type of anchovies become crispy when fried, different from the anchovies kept in brine and served with a salad or pizza, Mediterranean style. Dried anchovies come in different types and sizes. The whiter anchovy is better quality and hence more expensive. The best supplier of anchovies in Malaysia is Tanjong Dawai in the northern state of Kedah, two hours' drive from my home town in Penang. My late parents would drive all the way there to buy the best anchovies to serve at their canteen in Butterworth. To prepare the anchovies, take off the heads and split the fish in half to remove the gut. Wash them and dab dry with kitchen paper before frying them in vegetable oil until crispy. The fried anchovies can be kept in a jar for a few weeks and served as a condiment for coconut rice (see page 153).

Soy Sauce
KICAP MASIN

Soy sauce comes in different colours, from light to dark. The one I recommend for the kitchen cupboard is light soy sauce, which is thinner than the darker version. Dark soy sauces are fermented for longer, and caramel is sometimes added. Light soy sauce, however, is good for seasoning, without changing the colour of your dish. To make a dish which requires fish sauce vegetarian, replace the fish sauce with soy.

Sweet Soy Sauce
KICAP MANIS

Not many people are aware of the availability of sweet soy sauce on supermarket shelves. One of the best uses for it is in my special beef in soy sauce (see page 100). It's my all-time favourite. The soy sauce is made from soya beans, fermented with yeast, and with added sugar and spices. Apart from the rich, caramelized taste, sweet soy sauce is normally a lot thicker and darker compared to the salted soy sauce above. Once opened, cover the bottle top with clingfilm, to avoid leaks, and keep in the fridge. The shelf life for soy sauce is normally between one and two years, but if it smells or tastes slightly sour it is not fresh any more and should be discarded.

Dark Coconut Sugar
GULA MELAKA

Malaysian dark coconut sugar is different from the lighter-coloured palm sugar, which is more readily available. The authentic and original sugar, without any additional white sugar, turns mushy when crushed. Unfortunately much of the *gula melaka* that is available in the shops has had white sugar added, and you can tell this by its texture, which turns gritty when crushed. The sugar is made from coconut sap, which is collected and then cooked until it has reduced and turned into sugar. It is then poured into a bamboo mould to form cylinder-shaped blocks, about 8cm high. If you can't find dark coconut sugar, you can use molasses sugar as an alternative.

Banana Leaves
DAUN PISANG

Banana leaves are not edible. They are used to wrap food because of the aroma they impart, and are one of the traditional Malaysian ways of cooking (other methods use taro and bamboo leaves). When using banana leaves, it is a good idea to glaze the leaf over a low heat in order to make it smoother and more flexible. Otherwise it will be slightly brittle and easily torn when folded.

Puréed Herbs in Jars

My own range of jars will come in handy if you can't find all the ingredients you need for cooking Malaysian dishes. Chillies, ginger, turmeric, galangal, lemongrass, ginger flower, shallots and garlic – a complete set of the essential ingredients for Malaysian cooking. You can purchase them online from my website, www.normanmusa.com, or from the shops listed on the website.

My Spice Rack

My kitchen is always full of spices. Although I have one set of knives, which travels with me around the world for work, when it comes to spices I have to keep them ready in each of my three kitchens, in London, Manchester and Kuala Lumpur. When travelling in the UK I carry a round spice tin which contains seven small metal bowls, but I always have to remind my staff to stuff the bowls with kitchen paper, otherwise the spices spill in transit and get jumbled up, like an all-spice mix. For Malaysian cooking I recommend that you have seven main spices: coriander, cumin, fennel, cardamom, star anise, cinnamon and cloves. However, for a proper Malaysian store cupboard I suggest more variety, to cover all eventualities.

Coriander Seeds
BIJI KETUMBAR

Coriander seeds work as a base for a typical ground spice mix, just as onion or shallots work for a paste, and are used more than any other spice. The seeds have a lemony, citrusy and nutty flavour and a hint of spicy heat. It is best to dry-toast them, then grind and use them straight away. Ground seeds that are left for a long time quickly lose their flavour.

Cumin
JINTAN PUTIH

As I am a self-taught chef and learned to cook only after I moved to the UK, I am more familiar with the English names for spices. I find it confusing, as in Malay cumin is known as 'white seeds' though the colour is darker than fennel seeds, which are known as 'sweet seeds'. Cumin has a strong earthy flavour and aroma, and if you add too much it will make your dish bitter. It works best with strong-flavoured meat like beef, lamb and venison.

Fennel Seeds
JINTAN MANIS

These seeds look very similar to unpeeled rice grains, greenish in appearance and with an aniseed aroma and flavour. Fennel works best with seafood, or ground with other spices to make a mix for curries.

Green Cardamom
BUAH PELAGA

I hate it when I accidentally bite on a cardamom pod in a curry or rice dish. They are very unpleasant to chew because of their bitter and stale flavour. I receive many complaints about them from my restaurant customers! But they bring such a flavour boost. For a big batch of my popular beef in soy sauce (see page 100), I recommend that my staff make a pouch out of muslin to put the cardamom pods in, which makes it easier for them to remove them once the dish is cooked. Cardamom pods come in three colours – black, green and white. Green is the one commonly used in Malaysian cooking. I don't bruise or crush the pods before adding them to curries or rice, as that releases a stronger flavour, which can be overpowering.

Star Anise
BUNGA LAWANG

This was one of my mum's favourite spices. She kept it in an airtight jar and it lasted for years. It is used in most Malaysian curries, and gives a good balance of aromatic aniseed flavour and sweetness to curry dishes and rice. It works best with recipes that need simmering for a long time, like chicken rendang (see page 109) and my beef in soy sauce (see page 100).

Cinnamon Sticks
KULIT KAYU MANIS

The difference between cinnamon bark and stick is that the bark is peeled from the outer layer of the tree trunk whereas the stick is taken from the inner bark, which is more expensive. In my experience, cinnamon sticks from Sri Lanka are the best – they are so delicate and brittle, made from a few thin layers of the inner bark. The sticks produce a more delicate cinnamon essence, whereas the bark, which is obviously cheaper, is very woody and hard. If you are making your own ground spice mix and need to grind the cinnamon, I recommend you use cinnamon stick rather than bark. The smell of cinnamon can also drive away flies. Soak half a cinnamon stick in a small jar of water and leave in your kitchen.

Cloves
BUNGA CENGKIH

These are dried flower buds that can be used whole or ground. Their shape is like a spike with a round top, about 1cm long. Cloves have a sweet and aromatic flavour and are used in curries and also to infuse rice. Their spicy fragrance and intense flavour can be overpowering if used too much. Cloves are also good for numbing toothache: pound them to a powder and rub directly on to your gums.

Fenugreek
HALBA

These hard, bitter seeds have a lot of health benefits, and they are also one of the key ingredients in the ground spice mix for traditional fish curry (see page 73). Their strong smell is their most significant quality, but they are bitter in taste. Fenugreek is also added to rice to enhance the aroma and flavour. Drinking a glass of water with fenugreek soaked in it overnight can help with diabetes by lowering blood sugar levels.

Nutmeg
BIJI PALA

Nutmeg was once involved in a bloody war in South-east Asia, when a battle took place between the Dutch and the inhabitants of the Banda Islands, where nutmeg was found. In Malaysia, the trees are grown on Penang Island; the flesh is used for juice, as well as being pickled, while the mace and seed are used for cooking. I only use a small amount of freshly grated nutmeg in my cooking, as it is a more subtle spice.

Black & White Peppercorns
BIJI LADA HITAM DAN PUTIH

Black and white peppercorns actually come from the same seeds, the only difference being that with white peppercorns the outer skins are removed down to the smooth white under-layer before drying. I prefer to use white pepper in my cooking, as it gives a milder flavour. Before the Portuguese introduced chillies to Asia, peppercorns were used as the spicy heat ingredient.

Ground Turmeric
SERBUK KUNYIT

I honestly prefer to use fresh turmeric (see page 238) in my curries, but ground turmeric is handy if you can't find the fresh variety (though it is becoming more widely available in the UK these days). When selecting ground turmeric, try looking for the brightest yellow colour, as that defines its freshness.

Ground Mixed Spices for Meat & Seafood
REMPAH RATUS

These are my own blends of spices, designed for meat or seafood, that are available online from my website, www.normanmusa.com. The spice mixes are manufactured in Malaysia according to my recipe. The ground spice mix for seafood is a lot stronger in fennel, with a hint of fenugreek, which gives an aromatic flavour. The ground spice mix for meat has cumin and fennel added, to give an earthy aniseed flavour.

1   Cloves
2   Green Cardamom
3   Nutmeg
4   Chilli Flakes
5   Mustard Seeds
6   Fennel Seeds
7   Star Anise
8   Fenugreek
9   Cumin
10 Black Peppercorns
11 Halba Campur
12 Candlenuts
13 Cinnamon Sticks
14 Coriander Seeds

Herbs & Vegetables

Fresh herbs are as important in Malaysian cuisine as spices, but unfortunately some of them are not available in the UK, such as ginger flower and turmeric leaves (though ginger flower is included in my range of jarred products, see page 234). On the whole it is the leafy parts of the herbs, or the roots that are used in Malaysian cooking, and many of these have been scientifically proven to have medicinal and health benefits. I have listed here all the essential herbs that are required for my recipes. You can freeze most of them if you have any left over.

Bird's-eye Chillies
CILI PADI

These are the small, fiery chillies that are often added to traditional dishes such as grilled beef in turmeric and coconut milk (see page 106) or made into a *sambal*. They come in green and red varieties. They are a popular ingredient in traditional Malay cuisine in Negeri Sembilan, an area known for its centuries-old heritage food. To reduce their heat, simmer the chillies for a long time when using them in cooking. They also have antioxidant qualities.

Chillies
CILI MERAH

There is a bit of a debate about which is hotter, red or green chillies. Green ones tend to be hotter because they are less ripened and therefore less sweet, but I am reliably informed that the variety of chilli has a bigger impact on its heat than its colour does. If you want to reduce the heat of chillies, remove the seeds and just use the outer flesh.

Fresh Turmeric
KUNYIT HIDUP

Turmeric is a root from the same family as ginger. Although best known in dried powder form (see page 236), the fresh root is becoming increasingly available in good supermarkets and Asian shops these days. I prefer the fresh root to the dried powder because it gives a fresher, aromatic flavour and is more authentic. But don't worry if you can't find it. One teaspoon of powder is the equivalent of 2.5cm of fresh root, roughly. You need to peel the root in much the same way as you would ginger. Watch out – your fingers will go yellow but you can remove the stain by rinsing them with rice vinegar.

Fresh Ginger
HALIA

There are many ginger species, and most gingers that are available in the UK market are imported from China. In Malaysia we like to use young ginger, which is less fibrous than the older ginger you generally find in the UK. The best way to peel the root is to scrape the skin with the end of a teaspoon. The best-quality ginger in Malaysia can be found in Bentong, in the Cameron Highlands, where the soil and climate are perfect for producing the most spicy and aromatic roots.

Fresh Galangal
LENGKUAS

Another member of the ginger family, galangal is more peppery in taste and citrusy in aroma. Malaysian galangal is more pungent and pink in colour than mass-produced galangal imported from neighbouring countries such as Thailand. You can pick it up fresh in oriental stores or, failing that, you can find it in major supermarkets, ready-puréed in jars or dried in packets.

Lemongrass
SERAI

Often grown in the gardens of village homes, lemongrass is a staple ingredient in most Malay dishes. In its freshest form, picked from the garden, you can squeeze out its juice. To prepare the stalks, trim the ends and just use the central, less fibrous part of the grass. These days in supermarkets you can pick up lemongrass fresh or already puréed in a jar.

Garlic
BAWANG PUTIH

Garlic is used in many Chinese Malaysian stir-fries. It is used as a principle ingredient, before adding the meat or vegetables, whereas in Malay or Nyonya cooking it is used as a minor ingredient, after shallots or chillies. Pounding garlic using a pestle and mortar is the best way to release the juice and bring out the garlic flavour.

Onion
BAWANG BESAR

Onion acts as a base for spice curry pastes. When onion is mentioned in my recipes it means the white onions that are easily available. In Malaysia, *bawang besar* refers to red onions. Many of my recipes suggest you use shallots, but if you don't have them you can use onions instead.

Shallots
BAWANG MERAH

I suggest you use banana shallots, which you can easily pick up in a supermarket; however, if you can find the little Thai shallots in an Asian or oriental store, these are more authentic. Soak the shallots in warm water for 5 minutes – this makes them easier to peel. If a recipe calls for ready-made fried shallots, you can buy these in oriental stores.

Curry Leaves
DAUN KARI

Fresh is always best, and you can often pick these leaves up in Asian shops, and sometimes in major supermarkets. If you can't find them, use dried ones or even bay leaves. Fresh curry leaves can be frozen if you don't use a whole packet.

Pandan Leaves
DAUN PANDAN

Nutty and aromatic in flavour, pandan is often regarded as the vanilla of South-east Asia. The leaves are very versatile, and are used for their aroma and flavour but also for their natural green colour, which is popular in Malaysian sweets and desserts. For my curries, I prefer these to curry leaves, as they give a better, sweeter flavour. You can extract the natural green colour from pandan leaves by crushing them, soaking them in a little water, then sieving out the juice. I also dry them for making pandan and honey tea in my restaurant. You can often find pandan leaves in oriental stores; sometimes you will come across them frozen, and to make things easier pandan extract is also available in bottles. If you can't find the leaves or the extract, you can, depending on the recipe, try curry or bay leaves instead, although they will obviously give a different taste. For sweet dishes, you can substitute vanilla pods.

Kaffir Lime Leaves
DAUN LIMAU PURUT

Whether you find these frozen, dried or, if you're really lucky, fresh, kaffir lime leaves are available in oriental supermarkets and increasingly in major supermarkets and online. They have a wonderful lemony, intense fragrance and flavour. I prefer to shred mine very finely rather than put them into the dish whole, so that those sensual qualities are maintained and you get rustic strands of leaves in your curry, just like vanilla pod seeds in a dessert. If you can't find kaffir lime leaves, strips of lime rind make a good alternative.

Laksa Leaves
DAUN KESUM

Also known as polygonum leaves or Vietnamese coriander, *laksa* leaves are great for adding to soups, *laksas* and salads. These pungent, long, narrow pointed leaves are often found in Thai and Vietnamese shops, if you are lucky enough to have one locally. Like lemongrass, they are grown in village gardens back home in Malaysia, but here in the UK I have sometimes been able to buy them from a herb grower or specialist garden shop.

Ginger Flower
BUNGA KANTAN

Sometimes known as torch ginger, this is my all-time favourite, a unique Malaysian ingredient. Originating from a different variety but in the same family as common ginger, the buds are harvested before they open, ranging from white to dark pink shades, like longer-shaped tulips. Used in stews and soup-based recipes, ginger flower is especially famous in Nyonya cooking, and is also used in herb and rice salads. The flower has a unique subtle aroma and taste that is slightly floral, slightly gingery. It is difficult to get hold of in the UK, so I have included it in my range of jarred products, already puréed (see page 234). Lemongrass is a fragrant herb which, although citrusy, can be used as a substitute.

Coriander Leaves
DAUN KETUMBAR

Coriander leaves are great for garnishing, and I love using them to give herby freshness to appetizers. Chopped, they give added colour to main dishes when serving.

Pennywort
DAUN PEGAGA

Because of its health benefits you may have come across pennywort in tablet form in health food shops, but it is actually a popular herb in Malaysia and is normally eaten raw with a chilli dip. The round leaves give a delicate herby flavour to fresh salads. It is sometimes referred to as *gotu kola* in Indian circles. If you can't get pennywort in your local Asian store, you can use watercress as a substitute.

Thai Sweet Basil
DAUN KEMANGI

Thai basil is different from the Italian basil that is more easily found in your local supermarket. The purple stems and pointed leaves of Thai basil have an aniseed flavour, with a delicious sweetness and spicy edge. You can often find it in oriental shops and it can be used in stir-fries, curries, soups and salads.

Garlic Chives
KUCAI

This long green leaf looks very similar to a spring onion. It is different from the normal chives you can get in the supermarket. *Kucai* is long and flat and has a very strong garlicky smell and flavour. It is one of the key ingredients of Penang wok-fried flat noodles (see page 146). If you don't have garlic chives, use spring onion instead.

1 Laksa Leaves
2 Garlic Chives
3 Thai Sweet Basil
4 Mint Leaves
5 Pandan Leaves
6 Coriander Leaves

NORMAN MUSA is an award-wining Malaysian chef and the official Food Ambassador for Kuala Lumpur.

He is co-founder of Ning restaurant in Manchester and holds regular supper clubs in London. He also has a restaurant in Malaysia called Nasi Daging.

He regularly features in print media and has appeared on television on Tom Kerridge's *Best Ever Dishes* and *Sunday Brunch*. He is currently working on a cookery programme for Malaysian television. He regularly appears at food festivals around the UK, Europe and Malaysia. He also teaches regularly at cookery schools, like Leith's School of Food & Wine.

Index

S

Acknowledgements

The opportunity to write this wonderful book would not have come about without Sarah Randell, food director of Sainsbury's Magazine, who introduced me to my delightful book agent, Heather Holden-Brown. I thank you both.

To Rowan Yapp and the Square Peg team, thank you for allowing me to put my personal touch into every single aspect of this book.

To Andy, Anna, Annie, Kylee, Lucy, Stuart, Uyen, Jenny and India, you are the dream team! Thank you for putting up with my perfectionism.

A big thank you to all my friends – Ibby, Louise, Harri and my PA Nikesha – for your help throughout this amazing journey.

To Abang Lan and Kak Bariah, thank you for looking after me whenever I am in Malaysia.

To Puan Noraza Yusof, thank you for looking up to my talent and believing that I could carry out the ambassadorial role for the gastronomic city of Kuala Lumpur.

Finally to all my followers on social media, thank you for your support throughout the years.

----

9 8

Square Peg, an imprint of Vintage,
 20 Vauxhall Bridge Road,
London SW1V 2SA

Square Peg is part of the Penguin Random House group of companies
whose addresses can be found at global.penguinrandomhouse.com.

Penguin
Random House
UK

First published by Square Peg in 2016

www.penguin.co.uk/vintage

A CIP catalogue record for this book is available from the British Library

ISBN 9780224101547

Design by Anna Green at Siulen Design
Photography by Stuart Ovenden
Props styling by Kylee Newton
Food styling by Uyen Luu

Printed and bound in China by C&C Offset Printing Co.,Ltd

Penguin Random House is committed to a sustainable future for our business,
our readers and our planet. This book is made from Forest Stewardship Council®
certified paper.